W9-CPC-009

DESCENT³

OFFICIAL STRATEGY GUIDE

By Mark H. Walker
& Mike Emberson

||||IBRADYGAMES
TAKE YOUR GAME FURTHER™

Official DESCENT 3 Strategy Guide

LEGAL STUFF

Brady Publishing
An Imprint of
Macmillan Digital Publishing USA
201 W. 103rd St.
Indianapolis, IN 46290

ISBN: 1-56686-844-0
Library of Congress No.: 98-074954

Printing Code: The rightmost double-digit number is the year of the book's printing; the rightmost single-digit number is the number of the book's printing. For example, 99-1 shows that the first printing of the book occurred in 1999.

02   01   00   99   4   3   2   1

BradyGAMES Staff

Publisher
Lynn Zingraf

Editor-In-Chief
H. Leigh Davis

Title/Licensing Manager
David Waybright

Acquisitions Editor
Debra McBride

Creative Director
Scott Watanabe

Marketing Manager
Janet Eshenour

Assistant Licensing Manager
Ken Schmidt

Assistant Marketing Manager
Tricia Reynolds

Credits

Development Editor
David Cassady

Project Editor
Tim Cox

Screenshot Editor
Michael Owen

Copy Editor
Timothy Fitzpatrick

Book Designer
Donna Cambra

Production Designer
Dan Caparo,
Bob Klunder

TABLE OF CONTENTS

TELcom

About the Authors

Mark H. Walker

Mark would like to thank his wife Janice, Mike Emberson, Jeff Barnhart, and Debra McBride. In addition, a special thanks goes to Craig, Demian, and Andy from Outrage and to Paul Bodensiek for all their help.

Dedication:

For Meg and Bambi

Paul Bodensiek

Descent III is like a homecoming for Paul Bodensiek. He's already written books on Descent (for the PlayStation) and Descent II (for the PC). Descent was also the game that really got him hooked on 3D shooters. Before that, he was playing *Flight Simulator* and *X-Wing Fighter*.

On the rare occasions that he's not playing (or writing about) computer games, Paul builds web sites and does technical consulting through his company ParaGrafix.

Some of Paul's other game books include: *Complete Myst Hints and Solutions* and the *AOL Games Guide*. In addition, he's done the tech editing for a number of books, including the sections of this book that he didn't write.

His wife, Mary, and daughter, Melissa, now have a standing date on Wednesday nights while Paul immerses himself in *Half-Life* or *Jedi Knight* during his usual clan game. Thanks for being so understanding!

The return of Descent, and its great multiplayer options, has Paul lobbying the other members of the clan to change the game-of-choice.

Introduction

A plethora of games with 3-D graphics and 360-degree maneuverability fill today's store shelves. One of the true classics of this prevailing trend is *Descent*, the game made famous by the player's ability to rove underground, reveling in six degrees of stomach-knotting movement. With even more escape-level exploits in *Descent II*, the adrenaline rush continued. And now the third installment —*Descent 3*—is here, proceeding further with these labyrinth-like undertakings, not to mention some pretty cool above ground exploits.

The Game

Descent 3 brings more diversity to the *Descent* world than ever before. The goals and strategies are more varied and exciting. Each subterranean shaft now has a truly unique feel and look. In fact, the people at Outrage have done something extraordinary. You can now navigate your vessel out of the mines and into the rain and snow of other worlds.

But *Descent 3* doesn't stop there. Ten new weapons have been added to your arsenal, including a Napalm Cannon, a torch-thrower capable of roasting your enemies into a burnt crisp. Speaking of enemies, there are lots of them! Many of the Descent series' previous villainous robots return with the same relentless pursuit and precision, from the annoying Thiefbot to the sneaky Swatter, there will be plenty of mechanical machinations to keep your attention.

Multiplayer *Descent 3* is no slouch either. Sweep the corners of shafts to find your best friend nestled nearby, blast him to metal shards, and then revel in his (or her) defeat. Death Matching is great, but *Desent 3* also comes with several other multiplayer laser-fests including Team Anarchy, Hoard, and Capture the Flag. Couple all this with some warp-speed vertigo, and you have the latest installment in the *Descent* series.

Perhaps you thought there were only three dimensions in computer gaming. Guess again. *Descent 3* has added a few more. The zero-G travel of *Descent 3* has culminated in a computer gaming masterpiece with multi-feature improvements that will redefine the genre just as the original did several years ago. Buckle up pilots and get ready for the ride of your life!

The Book

Amidst all these new features, you will find plenty of excitement. However, we all know that shredding some Bot tin is the best way to have fun. This is, after all, why you bought the book. In this Official Strategy Guide, you will find essential tactics and tips that will make your journey less taxing and time consuming. Everything you need to know is right here at your fingertips.

Which weapons are best suited for each particular mission? Where are the enemy Bots stationed? How can you deactivate the force fields that block your path? What are these "hidden" levels your buddies keep talking about? The answers to these questions and much more are in this book. The following is a general listing of the different sections, and what each has to offer you.

The Introduction

This is, of course, where you are right now. This section contains a briefing on the game and discusses the layout of the book.

Chapter One:
Basic Piloting Strategies

Many a Descenter has become disoriented while traversing the infernal regions. This crash course on basic piloting skills will help you learn how to maneuver your way through the subterranean levels of *Descent 3* without confusion, making the cockpit and controls a lot less intimidating for those new to the *Descent* world.

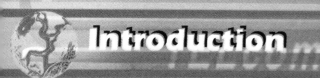

Chapter Two:
The Bad Guys & Other People

Are you ready to meet the guys who want to wreak havoc on your vessel's tunnel vision? Take a look at the pesky robots of the underworld, including such mechanical menaces as the Trackers, Gyros, Orbots, Swatters, Tubbs, and Thiefbots.

Chapter Three:
Weapons and Power-Ups

A hoard of new weaponry is at your disposal in this game. Statistics and other vital combat information accompany a list of weapons such as the Mass Driver, the Microwave Gun, and the Napalm Cannon.

Chapter Four:
The Missions

This is the *how-to* section of the book. Strategies for all 15 levels are provided (along with some "hidden" ones), including a detailed run-down on how to complete each mission successfully without ending up in fighter pilot heaven.

Chapter Five:
Multiplayer

So your best friends say they're experts on *Descent 3*? Well, invite them over and show 'em who's boss! See how that so-called expert handles a little Anarchy with this book in your corner. Hints for all four multiplayer games are provided here.

Chapter Six:
From the Horse's Mouth

Craig Derrick, the producer of *Descent 3*, gives us some inside scoop on how the game was created. This is your chance to find out what the Producer feels about the title.

Moving On

Now that you have an idea of what's in this book, let's head out and put it to use. To the land down under!

Chapter One: Basic Piloting Strategies

Okay, I know the rub. You didn't buy this book to listen to a middle-aged dweeb like myself preach piloting. You bought it for the walkthroughs. Nonetheless, I spent more than a few minutes flying the tunnels, corridors, and canyons of *Descent 3,* so perhaps I can fill you in on a couple of my better strategies. I can't promise that reading this will make you a subterranean Chuck Yeager, but I can promise that it will make you much better, much quicker than if you don't read it.

Get a Grip

Perhaps THE most important aspect of playing *Descent 3* well is configuring your controller properly. I guess it's possible to play with any configuration and controller, but it is certainly easier to play using the tried-and-true methods that follow.

Get a Stick

There is only one way to play *Descent 3* well—with a joystick. Don't waste your time with the keyboard, and by all means don't try to play it like *Quake II*—with a keyboard and mouse. A hatted joystick with a base-mounted throttle control and four to five buttons is your best option.

Button configuration is a personal choice, but I would seriously consider putting your "slide" functions on the hat and the afterburner button near your full throttle location.

> **Note**
>
> **A joystick with a throttle on the base is a dream, however, it isn't a requirement. I did a lot of my level crunching with a Thrustmaster Top Gun, using the "A," "Z," and "S" keys for throttle control.**

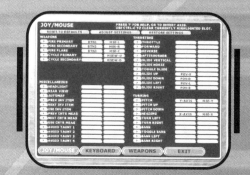

Tip

Yes, keyboard configuration is a personal choice, but I wouldn't waste the joystick buttons on inventory functions, such as selecting the next item in your inventory.

Get a Look

You can't destroy what you can't see, and you can't see what is hidden by glare. Take a moment to examine your monitor's position. If glare obscures the Squids attempting to waste your Pyro GL, then change the angle of the monitor or lower the light in the room.

Is it a big deal? No, but sometimes every little bit helps.

Get Some Game

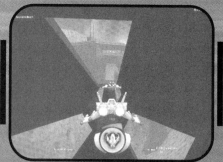

Descent 3 is a complex game. First-person shooters, like *Quake II*, are difficult, but *Descent 3* offers a third dimension to the equation—altitude. You not only have to look to the left, right, front, and back, but above and below. Sure, first-person shooters have their ledges and their grappling hooks, but you can't suspend yourself in mid-air. That is the difference, and the additional complexity, inherent in *Descent 3*.

Nevertheless, *Descent 3*'s complexity can be mastered. I only hope you master it more quickly with the following hints.

Basic Piloting Strategies

Get a Move On

Move out, pilot! To survive, you need to shuck and jive. You can't stay in one place for too long, because the computer AI is just too good in this game. The following are the different methods I use to stay out of trouble.

Move Slowly

Well, not usually. The "Move Slowly" header actually just checks the "Catchy Header" box in my author guidelines. Seriously, speed is not the only answer to your dogfight dilemmas.

Some bad Bots are much faster than your craft. The Starhawk, for example, will chew you up in open terrain. When fighting such Bots, it's best to slow down and use your superior turning ability to dodge incoming shots.

Tip

The Hood is another fast Bot. It is equipped with an experimental afterburner that accelerates its craft through a series of small explosions. Each explosion has a minimum burn time, so the Hood can't turn off its afterburner at will. Accordingly, you can lead the Hood in an afterburner-accelerated chase toward a solid wall, cut your afterburner at the last possible moment, and cut away from the wall. The poor Hood—without your craft's ability to quickly cut out its afterburner—will smash into the wall. What great fun!

Circle Strafe

This is a shooter standby if there ever was one. Stationary targets are easy to hit; but you already knew that. There are two types of movement that make a target dance in your sights: your craft's movement and your target's movement.

You can't do much about the second type of movement, however, you can control your craft's gyrations. Obviously, standing still is not in the equation. However, by sliding in the opposite direction to which you are turning, you can continue to move while maintaining a relatively stationary target picture in your sights (barring any radical movements by the target).

The Shuck and Shoot

Another good way to stay alive is to stay out of the enemy's line of sight. If they can't see you, they can't shoot you... Homing Missiles aside.

The Orbots and Squids are great at this game. They'll take a few shots and then duck behind a wall. It's a useful technique and one you should try yourself. Fire a few blasts (i.e. shoot), and then dive behind a wall or zip out of a door (i.e. shuck).

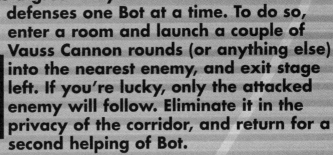

As a matter of fact, by learning an opponent's rhythm, you'll know when to shoot and when to shuck. For example, an Orbot shoots three blasts and then skitters around for approximately three seconds. You should shoot during this three-second period, and shuck while the Orbot is shooting.

The Bait and Switch

Some Bots (the Orbot and Gyro are good examples) are timid by nature. If there are two guarding a room, eliminate one and then launch a missile against the far wall to scare out the remaining Bot. Remember, you don't have to kill everything to win.

Similarly, coaxing (i.e. baiting) a Bot away from its pals is a great way to break down a room's defenses one Bot at a time. To do so, enter a room and launch a couple of Vauss Cannon rounds (or anything else) into the nearest enemy, and exit stage left. If you're lucky, only the attacked enemy will follow. Eliminate it in the privacy of the corridor, and return for a second helping of Bot.

Let Other Stuff Do Your Work

Face it, making it through some of these levels and eliminating some of these Bots is pretty tough. So why do it alone?

There are a few tricks that make the corridors seem a little less lonely. Read and learn.

-  **The Guidebot:** Use this little guy whenever possible. Need energy? Send your buddy out to find an energy source. Need a clue? Have the Guidebot lead you to the last marker you dropped. You did drop a marker, didn't you?

- **Mines:** One of the cool features of *Descent 3* are the Mines. Lace the entrance to a room with Mines, and then provoke the Bots. Stay inside the room and watch them swarm after you (and over the mines), obliterating themselves in the process. I love it when that happens.

- **Red Stinger:** Red Stingers are nasty, but they have an Achilles heel. It seems that they have a problem distinguishing friend from foe. If hit by another Bot's weapon discharge (even if it was formerly a friendly Bot), they will attack the offending machine until it is destroyed.

- **Barnswallows:** The Barnswallows' territorial tendencies make a German Shepherd look tame. The Swallows love to confiscate Power-Ups and will fight diligently to protect their nest of goodies. Hence, leading one flock of Barnswallows into another flock's nest will often start a fight from which few will survive. And then you can sit back and watch the fireworks!

General Piloting Tips and Neat Tricks

Some tips and tricks don't lend themselves to neat categorization. Such is the case with the following section. From energy management to napalm dripping techniques, there are plenty of tips in the following section.

Energy Management

Energy is a finite resource. Many Bots spew energy stars when destroyed, and there are energy recharge stations in some of the levels. Still, it never seems to be enough.

Basic Piloting Strategies

To play well, you must learn to manage your energy. For example, avoid firing lasers at every sound, and avoid depressing the trigger button throughout a dogfight. Sure, use the ammo you need, but pick and aim your shots.

Tip

The best way to save energy is to shoot well. Play through the tutorial a few times before you start the actual game. The more frequently your shots connect, the less shots you'll have to fire.

Tip

Shooting a Stormtrooper square in the head causes double damage. You can frequently take down these bad guys with one head shot if your aiming is correct.

Aim at the Tailbots' arms to destroy them, which in effect disarms the Tailbot. Unfortunately, it will grow them back.

Shield Management

You don't have to fight every Bot you see. Sometimes, discretion is the better part of valor. Use the techniques cited earlier to trick Bots away from rooms with lots of Shield Power Ups they may be guarding, and then zip into the space and absorb the shield orbs.

Tip

We all know that the Fixer Bot repairs your enemies. However, did you know that if you are very still, the Fixer will repair your craft's shields?

Limit the number of enemies that you engage at one time. You don't win style points for fighting fair, so look for ways to fight your enemies one Bot at a time.

It's a Three-Dimensional World

Don't forget the height factor. Many (heck, most) weapons, ammo, and Power-Ups are located near the ceiling. So don't forget to look up when you enter a room!

Tip

As a matter of fact, most good stuff is not only located near the ceiling, but in out-of-the-way places. One of the favorite locations seems to be just above a door. This makes perfect sense; unobservant players will fly into a room and never stop to look above or behind them.

Outrage Makes the Coolest Weapons!

Some guns/missiles are not only lethal in combat, but also useful for other purposes. Consider the following:

- **The Guided Missile Switch Tripper:** Some rooms are just too hot to handle, yet they contain a "must-be-tripped" switch. Why not hang outside the room and fly a Guided Missile into the switch. Too cool!

- **The Napalm Gun/Missile:** You can destroy some bad guys with an indirect hit from the Napalm Gun or a Missile. Simply hit the ceiling in front of the unit you want to destroy, and the napalm will drip onto your target.

The Final Tip

All this information is great, but none of it will serve any use if you don't practice. The best way to become good—real good—is play a lot. But hey, there are worse ways to spend your time!

Chapter Two: The Bad Guys & Other People

Descent 3 is filled with an assortment of bad guys, many of which are robots. They range from the diabolical Hellion and Dragon to the harmless, and often humorous, Scrubber and Gadget. Organic life-forms are rare and, for the most part, indifferent. In fact, the mutant Nomads of Mars are the only dangerous beings of this kind. Humans are, of course, your friends.

All of the personalities and life-forms in the *Descent* universe can be divided into four categories: Flyers, Walkers, Rollers, and Turrets. Flyers primarily navigate through the air, Walkers traverse by foot, Rollers use wheels for transportation, and Turrets include simple structures like cameras, missile launchers, etc. Here's the rundown.

Flyers

Flyers comprise the largest group of robots in the game. They are also one of the most diverse types of Bots. You have the bumblebee-zipping antics of the Orbot and Robo-Gerbil to dogfighters like the Starhawk and Hood. Even the freakish Nomads and monstrosities like the Homonculus are in this category.

Light Flyers

This batch of Flyers is typically small and fast. They range from the feisty and annoying Barnswallow Bots to the ordinary, feather-flapping Birds.

RAS-1 Gyro

-  **Family:** Security
- **Type:** Flyer
- **Class:** Light
- **Difficulty:** Low
- **Weapons:** One rapid-fire Level 1 Robot Laser

Description

The Gyro is a low-level security drone with minimal firepower.

Personality

Gyros are basically security guards, designed to stop unauthorized personnel from entering restricted areas.

Gameplay

They zip around and attack as soon as they catch the slightest glimpse or sound of an intruder. They tend to act timid when cornered alone, but when gathered together they stand their ground.

Tip

If the player is cloaked, s/he can sometimes catch the Gyro snoozing on the job. When sleeping, the player can poke the Bot without waking it. However, if you fire a weapon or de-cloak, the Gyro will immediately awaken and start to attack.

Drops

Energy and Shields.

The Bad Guys & Other People

O-2 Orbot

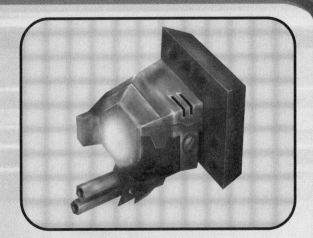

- 🜨 **Family:** Security/Level 1
- 🜨 **Type:** Flyer
- 🜨 **Class:** Light
- 🜨 **Difficulty:** Moderate
- 🜨 **Weapons:** Microwave Cannon

Description

The Orbot is one of the most difficult flyers to shoot down because of its speed and weaponry.

Personality

Somewhat similar to a hyperactive bumblebee.

Gameplay

The Orbot's quirky flight patterns and zipping speed force most players into a dogfight.

Tip

When hit with the Napalm Thrower or Napalm Rocket, the Bot's faulty thermal insulation forces it to burn at twice the normal damage rate. The Microwave Cannon actually overheats the droid instantaneously, turning the Orbot into mere vapor.

Drops

Shields, Energy, and Concussion Missiles.

SPT-99 Hunter

- **Family:** Security/Secret Level 2
- **Type:** Flyer
- **Class:** Light
- **Difficulty:** High
- **Weapons:** Robot Microwave and Robot Self-Destruct

Description

This dark, egg-shaped craft with large red eyes is the ultimate all-purpose security drone. Given the classified nature of the Hunter, a self-destruct mechanism is employed to prevent recovery of its secret technology.

Personality

A Peeping-Tom camera that will do anything to keep its eye on you. It is also in charge of alerting other security Bots of intruders.

Gameplay

If you don't kill the Hunter with one shot, it will detonate. Upon detonation, it will flail deadly shrapnel about.

Tip

If you shoot the Hunter with an EMD Gun, its electro-magnetic effects will activate the droid's self-destruction mechanism, setting off a Frag Missile.

Drops

Shields, Energy, Microwave Cannon, and Frag Missiles.

MY-4 Barnswallow

- 🜂 **Family:** Military
- 🜂 **Type:** Flyer
- 🜂 **Class:** Light
- 🜂 **Difficulty:** Low
- 🜂 **Weapons:** Two Level 3 Robot Lasers

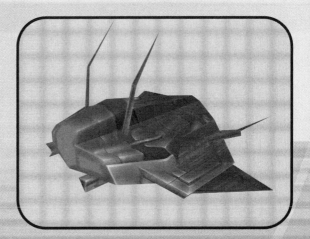

Description

Assisting units with re-arming duties, the Barnswallow is a multi-purpose drone used to salvage unused goods and supply them to other Bots.

Personality

Quick and hostile.

Gameplay

The Barnswallow's job consists of collecting available weapons and Power-Ups. Although this scavenger cannot fire when carrying an item, it will fight to its death if you swipe one of its cherished objects.

Tip

Barnswallows are territorial creatures. Sometimes two groups of these tin critters will hide out in a room.

Drops

Shields, Energy, and whatever it's carrying.

The Bad Guys & Other People

KB-50 Sharc

- 🜨 **Family:** Military/Level 13
- 🜨 **Type:** Flyer
- 🜨 **Class:** Light
- 🜨 **Difficulty:** Low
- 🜨 **Weapons:** Rapid Bite

Description

The Sharc is designed to guard perimeters from enemy trespass.

Personality

Sharcs are erratic, easily provoked, and not too bright by AI standards.

Gameplay

With their shark-like jaws and movement, these flyers love to take a bite out of their enemies.

Tip

Sharcs are dumb! If you enter a room and don't touch or shoot them, they more often than not will let you pass unscathed. Sometimes, they will even pursue Guided Missiles and Seeker Mines thinking they are food. Usually, the Sharc will swallow the projectile only to burp up the explosion unharmed. On occasion, though, the Sharc is unable to expel the projectile, resulting in its cataclysmic death.

Drops

Shields and Energy.

Bird

- 🔹 **Family:** Special-Ambient-Organic
- 🔹 **Type:** Flyer
- 🔹 **Class:** Light
- 🔹 **Difficulty:** Low
- 🔹 **Weapons:** None, technically

Description

These creatures circle the skies looking for Hoppers below.

Personality

Exhibits all of the typical characteristics of a bird.

Gameplay

Avoid the Birds if at all possible. Colliding with one usually results in minor shield damage, while smacking into a flock can even cause an engine fire.

Tip

If one of these feathered creatures gets close enough to a Hopper, it will swoop down and swallow the little lizard. Cool, huh?

Drops

Nothing.

The Bad Guys & Other People

Nomad

- **Family:** Special-Ambient-Organic
- **Type:** Flyer
- **Class:** Light
- **Difficulty:** Low
- **Weapons:** Variable, low-level weapons by type

Description

Nomads are the survivors of the first Martian colony, mutated from a massive radioactive meltdown. The CED's sabotaging of atmosphere processors caused the meltdown of the PTMC colony, which in turn has created this mysterious race.

Personality

These semi-human/semi-machine creatures act unfriendly towards trespassers.

Gameplay

Like Frankenstein's monster, Nomads dislike fire. In fact, they are susceptible to fire-based attacks, which cause double damage.

Tip

More accustomed to dark environments, Nomads flee into the shadows when exposed to light.

Drops

Energy and Shields.

Medium Flyers

The Medium Flyers generally have more bulk, both in character and size. In fact, some of the most interesting robot personalities are in this group, like the klepto-maniacal Thief Bot, the friendless bully RAS-2 Tubbs, or the pistol-packing Gunslinger.

RAS-2 Tubbs

- 🌀 **Family:** Security
- 🌀 **Type:** Flyer
- 🌀 **Class:** Medium
- 🌀 **Difficulty:** Moderate
- 🌀 **Weapons:** Melee Attacks (punch & backhand)

Description

The Tubbs does not fire projectiles. However, its brute strength enables it to knock out opponents faster than any Heavyweight Champion.

Personality

Tubbs is an arrogant bully. It will often rush toward you without care or concern about its own mortality. Because it refuses to call for backup from other Bots, poor Tubbs is usually restricted to fighting alone.

Gameplay

Tubbs is one of those enemies that must be killed. If not, it will continue to corner you until it pummels your spacecraft into the ground.

Tip

Poor ol' Tubbs is a lonely robot! If you offer it a Power-Up as it advances, Tubbs will examine the gift for nearly 10 seconds in sentimental gratitude before resuming its boxing routine.

Drops

Shields and Energy.

SK-I Sickle

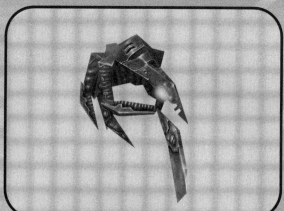

- **Family:** Security

- **Type:** Flyer

- **Class:** Medium

- **Difficulty:** Low

- **Weapons:** Melee attacks (sickle slash and tail whips); the tail-stun attack is peculiar in that it drains about 10 Energy points and all of the player's Afterburner reserves.

Description

The "Reaper" was designed for security duty in hazardous facilities.

Personality

Any Bot that resembles a cross between a maggot, bat, and the Grim Reaper is best left to itself.

Gameplay

Sickles are populous in large rooms where they can attach to the ceiling and sleep like bats. If they sense an intruder's presence, they quickly attack the invader with their scythe-like appendages.

Tip

Torching Sickles with the Napalm Gun is the most efficient method in eradicating these pests from their slumbering existence.

Drops

Energy and Shields.

M-1 Manta Ray

- **Family:** Military/Level 9
- **Type:** Flyer
- **Class:** Medium
- **Difficulty:** Moderate
- **Weapons:** EMD Gun

Description

The Manta Ray is a bomber specifically designed to raid enemy ground forces.

Personality

A graceful peace of work that lacks speed and maneuverability.

Gameplay

Although it doesn't maneuver well in combat, the Manta Ray has an electro-magnetic shield that repels approaching enemies. Not only does the shield shock its opponent, it can also ricochet particle weapons like the Vauss and Mass Driver.

Tip

Because the Manta Ray uses a shielding device similar to the Omega Cannon, the player can attack with his or her Omega Cannon, creating a weird side effect. The Omega Cannon transfers twice the amount of Shields from the Manta Ray to you, throwing your spacecraft from the bomber. If the Manta Ray is destroyed as a result of this Shield loss, it will explode after you have been hurled out of range.

Drops

Energy, Shields, Plasma Cannon, and Concussion Missiles.

BDC-100 Stormtrooper

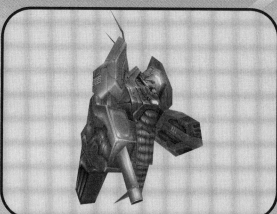

- **Family:** Military/Level 12
- **Type:** Flyer
- **Class:** Medium
- **Difficulty:** High
- **Weapons:** Regular Troopers have Robot Vauss and Robot Impact Mortar; Special Troopers have Robot Napalm and Robot Impact Mortar; Lieutenants have Robot Mass Driver and Robot Impact Mortar

Description

Including an array of other models (Flametrooper, Omegatrooper, and Leadtrooper), the Stormtrooper series is one of the most formidable CED flying machines.

Personality

Specializing in close combat, this craft is noted for its precision targeting.

Gameplay

When fighting alone, Stormtroopers revert to sniping at their opponents.

Tip

A Stormtrooper's head is its Achilles' heel. If shot in the noggin, the craft suffers double damage.

Drops

Energy, Shields, Robot Vauss or ammunition, Robot Napalm Thrower or ammunition, Robot Mass Driver or ammunition.

The Bad Guys & Other People

SQ-90 Squid

- **Family:** Industrial
- **Type:** Flyer
- **Class:** Medium
- **Difficulty:** Low
- **Weapons:** Plasma Cannon

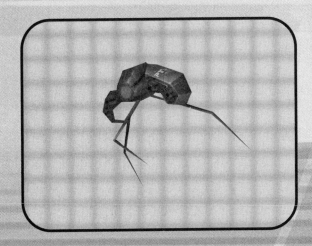

Description

Squids are used for maintaining electrical cables.

Personality

Drifting craft.

Gameplay

The Squid has an assortment of characteristics. First, it's immune to all energy-based attacks, except those of the Vauss, Mass Driver, and Missiles/Mines. Second, if you touch the vessel, the Squid will drain some of your energy, knocking you back in the direction from which you came. The SQ-90 is also armed with a Laser Cannon, but will not fire unless attacked first.

Tip

The Squid uses energy fired at it to increase the power of its lasers.

Drops

Shields and Energy.

The Bad Guys & Other People

RR-47 Tailbot

- **Family:** Industrial
- **Type:** Flyer
- **Class:** Medium
- **Difficulty:** Moderate
- **Weapons:** EMD Gun

Description

These tough, industrial flyers are known for their regenerative properties. The PTMC supposedly has programmed a procedural Virus on the Tailbot that will enable it to regenerate wounded parts.

Personality

The Tailbot is one of the most spiteful machines of the *Descent* legions, because it sometimes picks a fight with other Bots.

Gameplay

Your typical fighting machine, this Bot occasionally employs a sneak attack with its red tail.

Tip

You can blow off the Tailbot's arms with a Level 4 Laser (or better). Unfortunately, the appendages will grow back within 5 seconds.

Drops

Shields, Energy, Vauss Cannon or ammunition.

ARC-12 Sparky

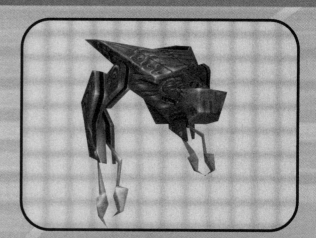

- **Family:** Industrial
- **Type:** Flyer
- **Class:** Medium
- **Difficulty:** High
- **Weapons:** Melee Attack (drains energy; secondary attack prevents player from switching weapons of any kind for 5-10 seconds)

Description

Old four eyes utilizes its welding skills for maintenance and salvage duties. The Sparky has been known to experience some problems with its guidance systems, creating massive mechanical failures.

Personality

A tenacious and sneaky foe.

Gameplay

The Sparky attacks with its electrical arc welder and sometimes with its claws. The claws acutally lock onto its enemy's weapon-selection capabilities for several seconds.

Tip

If you circle the Sparky, causing it to track your fighter for two complete revolutions, the confused Bot will twirl until it spews sparks and explodes.

Drops

Energy and Shields.

The Bad Guys & Other People

OS-114 Old Scratch

- 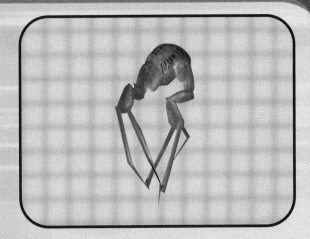 **Family:** Industrial
- **Type:** Flyer
- **Class:** Medium
- **Difficulty:** Moderate
- **Weapons:** Melee Attacks (swiping claw)

Description

Old Scratch, with its huge dangling claws, is one of the oldest robots in the PTMC's arsenal.

Personality

Indicative of its name, Old Scratch is a demonic machine. Evil and dangerous because of its regenerative abilities and relentless aggression, these craft can prevent an incredible obstacle when they attack in droves.

Gameplay

A group of Old Scratches usually surround and attack their prey. However, if its Shields are severely depleted, it will retreat until they regenerate.

Tip

Old Scratch is a fighter to the end. Occasionally, when wounded, it will lunge at a player and rip his or her weapons off the ship.

Drops

Shields and Energy.

G7-II Thief

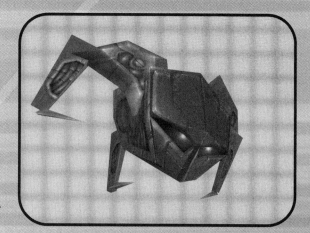

- **Family:** Special-Industrial

- **Type:** Flyer

- **Class:** Medium

- **Difficulty:** High

- **Weapons:** Special occasion only (features Robot Self-Destruct and Robot Proximity Mine)

Description

Once designed to remove rubble for general mining labor, this green-colored Thief now suffers from a viral infection that compels it to swipe goods from the arsenals of others.

The Bad Guys & Other People

Personality

Sometimes funny, but always clever, this Bot will gladly pick your pockets. A kleptomaniac in nuts-and-bolts form, the Thief is a sneaky coward that will steal your weapons at the most inopportune times.

Gameplay

One of the most annoying robots in the *Descent* universe, the Thief never runs out of tricks to get its nasty paws on your inventory.

The Thief has an arsenal of tactics. Some of them include: reaching into its belly to pull out and drop a Proximity Mine; pressing a button on its head and Cloaking; giving up and apologetically dropping the stolen goods only to self-destruct; creating additional likenesses of itself via Hologram; and kidnapping your Guidebot.

Drops

Energy, Shields, and Stolen Goods.

6-06 Gunslinger

- ⚙ **Family:** Industrial
- ⚙ **Type:** Flyer
- ⚙ **Class:** Medium
- ⚙ **Difficulty:** Moderate
- ⚙ **Weapons:** White Lasers

Description

This broad-shouldered, greenish-gray, torso-like robot with horns is "wanted" for its coordination skills, quick reflexes, and firing precision.

Personality

Like the Duke himself, this Bot is cool under fire, ready to light you up with its big gun barrels.

Gameplay

Often seen twirling its guns, the Gunslinger will not fire unless fired upon first. But beware: its pistol shots rarely miss.

Tip

If you kill the Gunslinger with a weapon other than a Laser, a little Gunboy will appear.

Drops

Energy, Shields, and Lasers.

The Bad Guys & Other People

Heavy Flyers

Big, bad, and dangerous! This is one motley band of ugly machines, from the vacuum-sucking mouth of the Excavator to the Battle of the Bots champion, Dravis' very own OD-9 Dragon.

RAS-3 Stinger

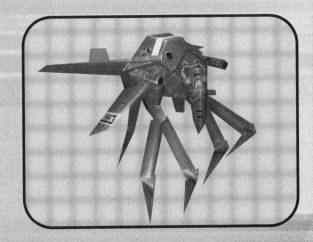

- **Family:** Security/Level 3
- **Type:** Flyer
- **Class:** Heavy
- **Difficulty:** High
- **Weapons:** Homing Missiles

Description

This heavily armored, wasp-like robot has red and blue flashing lights, which suits a machine built for policing purposes. The Stinger, however, has problems with its IFF recognition program, causing problems in its identification of friendly and enemy units.

Personality

Can anyone say *police brutality*? The Stinger is the largest and most aggressive of all security flyers.

Gameplay

The RAS-3 hates to let an interloper get away. It will use its Robot Afterburner to intercept security violators in flight.

Tip

Due to the IFF glitch, if the Stinger accidentally gets hit by another robot, it will attack the Bot and pursue it until the attacker is destroyed.

Drops

Shields, Energy, Vauss Cannon, and Frag Missiles.

MF-8 Hood

-
- **Family:** Military/Level 14

- **Type:** Flyer

- **Class:** Heavy

- **Difficulty:** High

- **Weapons:** Two Robot Cyclone Missile Launchers; Two Level 4 Robot Lasers

Description

Resembling a floating iron hood, the MF-8 is used primarily for conquests involving other planets. Because it utilizes a new pulsed-burn Afterburner, the Hood can move faster than the Starhawk.

Personality

A very smart Bot, the Hood possesses instinctive hunting skills.

Gameplay

The Hood provides some of the hardest and longest dogfight scenarios in *Descent 3*. Its Robot Afterburner and use of Chaff add to the difficulty.

Tip

To exploit the MF-8's Afterburner, coax the flyer into using it, and then dive toward a wall, building, or hillside before pulling up at the last moment. Now look back to see the newly formed Hood ornament on that particular structure.

Drops

Shields, Energy, Cyclone Missiles, and Lasers.

SH-1100 Thresher

- **Family:** Industrial/Level 7
- **Type:** Flyer
- **Class:** Heavy
- **Difficulty:** High
- **Weapons:** Twin Fusion

Description

The Thresher is a large, orange robot with a hammerhead and large claws.

Personality

A powerful Bot with little regard for smaller adversaries.

Gameplay

The Thresher loves to charge its opponents. It's best to stay away from this monstrosity and utilize ranged attacks, even if the Thresher resorts to its Mass Driver.

Tip

Oftentimes, the SH-1100 will try to impress its adversaries by picking up a crate and crushing it. If you fire upon the Thresher before it shreds the crate, it will angrily hurl it at you.

Drops

Energy, Shields, Mass Driver or ammunition.

The Bad Guys & Other People

OD-9 Dragon

- ⚙ **Family:** Boss-Military/Level 11
- ⚙ **Type:** Flyer
- ⚙ **Class:** Heavy
- ⚙ **Difficulty:** High
- ⚙ **Weapons:** Robot Napalm; Homing Napalm Rocket Blob Launcher; Quad rapid-fire burst Robot Level 1 Lasers; Grasping Homing Chain-Claws; Foreleg Talons Melee Attack

Description

An arachnid-like robot with Napalm Thrower mandibles and large thorny legs, the Dragon is one of Dravis' favorite pieces of machinery.

Personality

The OD-9 is a deadly killing machine that loves to toy with its opponents.

Gameplay

The Dragon expels a Homing Napalm Rocket Blob from its orifice when attacked. When you get too close to the orifice, the Dragon will shoot out flying pincers that will steal your inventory items. Sometimes the chain will drag your spacecraft into its orifice, consuming it in the process.

Tip

Don't shoot at the Dragon and avoid its chains. Try to launch an Impact Mortar round into the orifice of its abdomen. This will ignite the gases from its Napalm Blob Launcher, resulting in the destruction of the Dragon's abdomen. The torso will then detach from the abdomen, and eventually die. But beware: This monster still has plenty of fight in it. Take out the crawling torso with everything but Napalm-based weapons.

Drops

Energy, Shields, Napalm Thrower and ammunition, Lasers, and any stomach contents.

SX-66 Hellion

- 🌀 **Family:** Boss-Military/Level 15
- 🌀 **Type:** Flyer
- 🌀 **Class:** Heavy
- 🌀 **Difficulty:** Highest
- 🌀 **Weapons:** Robot Beam Weapon, Robot Mega Missile Launchers, Robot Frag Missiles

Description

The Hellion is large and spherical, with two long tentacles attached to its sides and a disk-like protrusion on its back. These creatures are to be unleashed upon Earth to destroy the planet's military capabilities. The Hellion also guards Dravis' Stronghold.

Personality

Big and bad, the Hellion gets furious when its offspring gets vaporized.

Gameplay

The SX-66 is one of the deadliest robots in the *Descent 3* universe. It has a multitude of weapons, including four tentacles that can fire clones of projectiles fired by the player, two tentacles used for slapping its opponent, and armor that's resistant to everything but Napalm weaponry.

Tip

It takes a considerable amount of time to cause much damage with Napalm. You can kill the Hellion by firing into the large cavern's ceiling, causing lava to seep down and destroy the beast. Because of its ability to create offspring, though, it is necessary to kill as many of its young as possible. For every three offspring killed, the Hellion loses a limb, starting with the clone-retaliation tentacles and ending with the two melee tentacles.

Drops

Energy, Shields, Mega Missiles, Mass Driver and ammunition.

The Bad Guys & Other People

U6-9 Super Thief

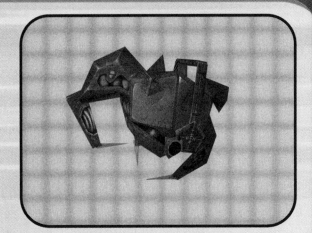

- ⚙ **Family:** Mini-Boss-Industrial/ Level 2

- ⚙ **Type:** Flyer

- ⚙ **Class:** Heavy

- ⚙ **Difficulty:** High

- ⚙ **Weapons:** Uses the weapons it steals

Description

Resembles the Thief Bot except it's larger and has weirder attachments.

Personality

The once ordinary Thief Bot is the victim of Dr. Sweitzer's Virus experiments. Because of this testing, the Bot's firing is often wild and erratic.

Gameplay

Once a thief, always a thief. This Bot is still full of lots of mischief, and can be as immoral as its little brother. You must kill this freak so you can retrieve the Sweitzer research files inside of it.

Tip

The Super Thief is really spaced out! If you reduce its Shields by more than 75 percent in less than 5 seconds, it will fly away until it floats off into space and explodes.

Drops

Energy, Shields, and Stolen Goods.

N-010 Homunculus

- **Family:** Boss-Industrial/Level 5

- **Type:** Flyer

- **Class:** Heavy

- **Difficulty:** High

- **Weapons:** An energy-draining tentacle-like arc; a large, hammer-like arm; a large claw arm; one large mouth bite attack; and Robot Seeker Mines

Description

The Nomads supposedly created this freak long ago. The creature is rumored to be a twisted, metal incarnation created from a junkyard of robot remains. It's also reported to have a large mouth with specialized tentacles.

The Bad Guys & Other People

Personality

The Homunculus is a ravenous beast with a huge appetite, ready to devour Energy, Shields, spacecraft, etc. It is also renown for its loud, ominous bellowing, which you can hear in areas near the creature's lair.

Gameplay

This horror loves to follow its prey at a distance, waiting for its prey to strike a dead end, at which point it attacks.

Tip

If you are Invulnerable when Homunculus bites you, it will suffer a substantial amount of damage. If you shoot it as it tries to gobble you up, the monster will instantaneously die.

Drops

Energy, Shields, and Seeker Mine packs.

Walkers

The Bad Guys & Other People

Walkers

Walkers are diverse, from the small lizard Hopper to the colossal Juggernaught. Although they move by foot, they don't always stay planted to the ground.

Light Walkers

This group consists of Humans, Hoppers, and Pests.

Human

- **Family:** Special-Ambient-Organic

- **Type:** Walker

- **Class:** Light

- **Difficulty:** Low

- **Weapons:** None

Description

People dressed in uniforms.

Personality

Humans are usually afraid of you and other robots.

Gameplay

It's wise not to kill the humans. They can lead you to places or reward you for protecting them. Furthermore, the game will penalize you for killing them.

Tip

Whether you kill a human accidentally or deliberately, the nearest matcen will automatically produce more robots to serve as punishment for your inhumanity!

Drops

Nothing.

The Bad Guys & Other People

PB-5 Pest

- 🌀 **Family:** Industrial
- 🌀 **Type:** Walker
- 🌀 **Class:** Light
- 🌀 **Difficulty:** Low
- 🌀 **Weapons:** Rapid-fire Level 1 Robot Laser

Description

The Pest is an arachnid-like robot designed to pick up garbage. It is similar to the spider, except it has four legs. The Pest also has pincers and a scorpion-like tail that contains a disintegrator beam.

Personality

Like a cockroach, this guy tends to shun the light, often hiding in the shadows of large caves and structures. On occasion, it will fire upon a player from behind and attack in large groups.

Gameplay

Fast as a cockroach, but as vulnerable as one too!

Tip

Truly, these creatures are garbage collectors, consuming their own dead.

Drops

Energy, Shields, and Lasers.

The Bad Guys & Other People

Heavy Walkers

Heavy Walkers are also rare, but they more than make up for their small number with their enormous size.

SW-9 Juggernaught

- 🔘 **Family:** Security/Level 10

- 🔘 **Type:** Walker

- 🔘 **Class:** Heavy

- 🔘 **Difficulty:** High

- 🔘 **Weapons:** Twin rapid-fire Robot Concussion Missiles; Twin Robot Vauss Cannons

Description

The Juggernaught is a large, bulky, four-legged walker with thick-plated armor. It is used primarily for surveillance in wilderness and perimeter terrain patrols.

Personality

The SW-9 may appear slow, but this Bot possesses a great deal of boldness and daring when it comes to toe-to-toe fighting.

Gameplay

This gargantuan of the *Descent* world is immune to Energy-based primary weapon attacks. However, the Juggernaut is susceptible to Missiles and other projectiles.

Tip

If you fire upon the Juggernaught's neck enough times, its head will fall off, disabling its Vauss Cannons.

Drops

Energy, Shields, Concussion Missiles, Vauss Cannons and ammunition.

M-80 Supertrooper

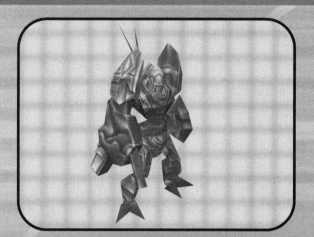

- 🔘 **Family:** Military/Secret Level 1

- 🔘 **Type:** Walker

- 🔘 **Class:** Heavy

- 🔘 **Difficulty:** High

- 🔘 **Weapons:** Turret-mounted Robot Microwave Cannon; Robot Cyclone Launcher

Description

Relatively humanoid in appearance, the Supertrooper is fast, durable, and notorious for its impressive jumping ability.

Personality

Think of a Stormtrooper on steroids.

Gameplay

The M-80 Supertrooper can damage its opponent by jumping onto its opponents' craft.

Tip

When in the air, hit it with a Mega Missile or Mass Driver to knock it down. It will take damage during its fall.

Drops

Energy, Shields, Microwave Cannon, and Cyclone Missiles.

Rollers

Rollers

It's time to rock 'n' roll with the likes of the Prowler and Flak. These guys are part of what I call the *Descent 3* Roller Derby.

Medium Rollers

Medium Rollers range from the meticulous Scrubber to the dune-buggy-like Prowler.

RM-10 Flak

- 🜨 **Family:** Military
- 🜨 **Type:** Roller
- 🜨 **Class:** Medium
- 🜨 **Difficulty:** Moderate
- 🜨 **Weapons:** Quad-alternating Robot Mass Drivers

Description

Although it resembles a tricycle, the Flak is a far cry from child's play.

Personality

Persistent in its pursuit of enemies, the RM-10 can be quite annoying.

Gameplay

Although this robot has a very long firing range, it also has one of the poorest targeting computers. Therefore, each time the Flak takes aim at its opponent, it must stop to fire.

Tip

Take it out with a Mass Driver to its rear tracks. The lightly armored treads make it easy to stop this pest in its tracks (so to speak).

Drops

Energy, Shields, Mass Driver and ammunition.

RM-15 Tracker

- ⚡ **Family:** Military
- ⚡ **Type:** Roller
- ⚡ **Class:** Medium
- ⚡ **Difficulty:** High
- ⚡ **Weapons:** Twin Robot Mega Missile Launchers

Description

A tank with large missile pods used in numerous combat situations.

Personality

Hesitant and dumb.

Gameplay

The RM-15 is slow to react, but when it does, it will shove more than a few Mega Missiles your way.

Tip

The Tracker has two primary weaknesses. First, its rear hull armor is thin. Second, you can put the Tracker out of commission by taking out its treads with a Mega Missile.

Drops

Shields, Energy, and Mega Missiles.

Turrets

Turrets

Turrets are guns mounted on objects such as walls and floors.

Light Turrets

The security area is covered in this category.

ST-55 Watcher

- **Family:** Special-Ambient-Security

- **Type:** Turret

- **Class:** Light

- **Difficulty:** Low

- **Weapons:** None.

Description

The Watcher is a surveillance camera mounted on a stalk. The Watcher can be mounted anywhere.

Personality

It likes to watch.

Gameplay

This camera Bot can be really snoopy.

Tip

You can interact with it by using the Watcher to see through other security camera lenses in the facility. Neat, huh?

Drops

Energy and Shields.

Medium Turrets

This category contains such hard-hitting Turrets as the MT-C3 Swatter and the MT-A1 Destroyer.

MT-AI Repeater/Destroyer

- **Family:** Military
- **Type:** Turret
- **Class:** Medium
- **Difficulty:** Low
- **Weapons:** Robot Vauss Cannon

Description

Repeaters, along with their big brother, Destroyers, are used as a perimeter defense system.

Personality

Small, swiveling turret that will boldly fire upon enemies.

Gameplay

Due to its speed and precision, the MT-A1 can take out its target with Vauss Cannon projectiles.

Tip

If you Cloak anywhere near the Repeater, its sensors will receive conflicting data, causing it to spin wildly and shoot erratically.

Drops

Shields, Energy, Vauss Cannon and ammunition.

Chapter Three: The Weapons of Descent 3

One of the neatest things about *Descent 3* is the incredible array of weapons. There are weapons to lase your enemies, roast your enemies, and fill your enemies full of metal analogy-type slugs. Sure, *Descent's* top-notch manual covers the weapons, but who wants a lapful of books while they're blasting through a PTMC prison? So, for your gaming convenience, we're including the weapons in this handy strategy guide.

Player Spacecraft

Although not considered a weapon per se, no one can deny that the game's three spacecraft are deadly machines. The following section describes each craft. Similar descriptions appear in Chapter Five, but for those who hate flipping pages I've also included the phraseology below.

Pyro GL

The latest Pyro model is one of the best all-around ships ever crafted for a *Descent* mission. Its combination of speed and firepower are enough to carry most gamers through all 15 levels. The Pyro's greatest strength is that it doesn't have a single great strength. You can dogfight, you can snipe from a distance, and you can change your strategy on the fly and exploit the weaknesses of your opponent.

At a Glance

- ⚙ Faster than previous Pyros

- ⚙ High turn rate

- ⚙ Great for sniping and dogfights

Magnum

Although the Magnum is somewhat slow, it is a devastating machine for close-combat scenarios. The Magnum has the toughest shields of any ship, and its weapons pack the biggest punch: the Microwave Cannon, Napalm Gun and Fusion all fire triple bursts instead of the usual two, and the Mass Driver has a quicker reload time. The Magnum can carry more ammo, and its Quad Lasers fire in a close, tight spread so all four are more likely to hit its target. However, the Magnum is a big, slow target without much pick-up in the afterburner department.

At a Glance

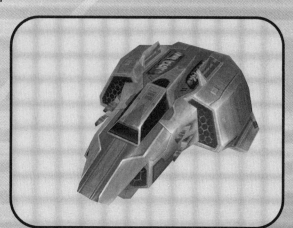

- Tough shields

- Offers more cargo space than the Phoenix or Pyro GL

- Shoots triple bursts with Microwave Cannon, Napalm Gun, and Fusion Cannon

Phoenix

The Phoenix is the quickest and most maneuverable of the player ships. In the hands of a highly skilled pilot, the Phoenix's natural speed and strong afterburner make it difficult to hit and impossible to catch. This ship was born to "triple chord," but it's not as impressive at soaking up damage. Its light shields and less potent weaponry is the price you pay for such eye-popping maneuverability. The Phoenix is perfect for circling dogfights and run-and-gun sneak attacks.

At a Glance

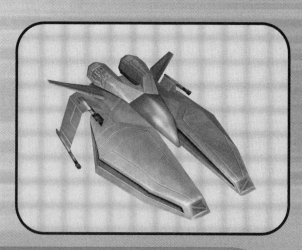

- Excellent for sneak-and-run attacks

- Strong afterburner feature

- Shielding is sacrificed for speed

- A strong ship for a strong pilot

The Weapons of Descent 3

Primary Weapons

Laser Cannon

Laser Cannons are standard combat issue for all Descenters. Although not the most powerful weapon, it can eliminate a Gyro just about as well as any other weapon. Additionally, the Laser Cannon doesn't use as much energy as some of the other implements of death.

At a Glance

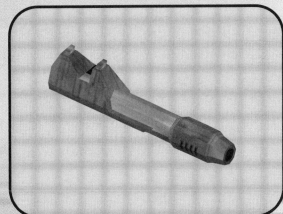

- Your basic energy-based weapon

- Uses twin turbo-lasers

- Easy on energy consumption

Super Laser

Think of the Super Laser as your Laser Cannon on steroids. You'll need this bigger laser for the larger Bots. This weapon inflicts more damage, but it also consumes more energy.

At a Glance

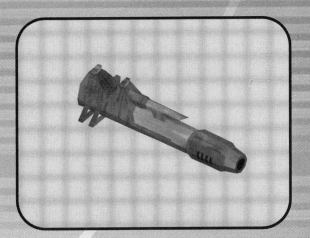

- High intensity weapon

- Quicker than its brother

- Spits out golden, twin turbo-lasers

- Uses more energy than its little brother

Vauss Cannon

A heavy cannon built with a high-caliber punch, the Vauss Cannon is perfect for shredding tin. Because it's a projectile weapon, it consumes no energy. That aspect, along with its macho sound, are special bonus perks.

At a Glance

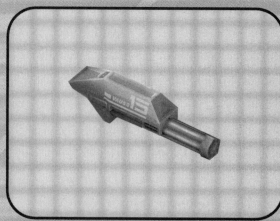

- Excellent for pummeling opponents with lead

- Features a rapid fire rate

- Doesn't consume energy

Mass Driver

Intended for sniper attacks, the Mass Driver is powerful and accurate. This is NOT the weapon of choice for clearing out a room of snarling Bots, but is great for taking out enemies from afar.

At a Glance

- Offers telescopic range

- Doesn't require many shots to take out enemies

Napalm Cannon

This incendiary weapon scorches Bots into a crisp. Although it lacks the range of lasers, Mass Drivers, or even the Vauss Cannon, its searing attacks prove devastating in close quarters.

At a Glance

- Spraying flames blanket lunging enemies

- Tailbots and Sickles succumb easily to its searing effects

EMD Gun

This super-charged energy weapon will "stun" your enemies.

At a Glance

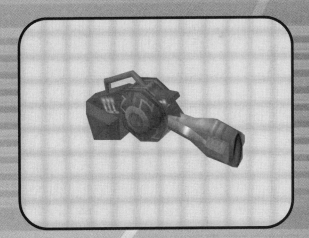

- Utilizes electro-magnetic dynamism for sizzling effects

- Rechargeable homing weapon

Microwave Cannon

The Microwave Cannon nukes Bots with heat waves of energy.

At a Glance

- Armor-plating buckles from the gyrating results

- Effects immobilize Bots, preventing them from returning fire while "stunned"

- The Orbot's weapon of choice

- Consumes lots of energy

Plasma Cannon

This weapon serves up rapid-fire volleys of accelerated plasma particles with deadly accuracy. The Plasma Cannon has good range coupled with a strong attack. This is one of the better weapons in your *Descent 3* arsenal.

At a Glance

- Fast and vicious attack

- Quickly puts most Bots out of commission

- Squids use a similar technology

- Good all-around weapon

Fusion Cannon

Utilizing purple globs of anti-matter, the Fusion Cannon draws in daredevil dogfighters like moths to a flame. The longer you hold the trigger, the more powerful the Fusion Cannon bolt. However, if you hold the trigger for too long, it causes damage to your shields.

At a Glance

- Ultimate overkill assault weapon

- A couple of twitches will dispose of the peskiest opponents

- Useful "dial a charge" trigger feature lets you build up the charge you need

Omega Cannon

This updated weapon peels away robot defense shields with devastating new energy-draining capabilities. It possesses a lethal attack, however, it's a real energy consumer. It also doesn't have much range.

At a Glance

- Its arcing stream of blue rays is excellent for attacking agile foes

- Capable of boosting your shields at the expense of your target's energy

- Short range

The Missile Things

Concussion Missile

As its name implies, the Concussion Missile can put a hurting on its target. This is the ubiquitous missile equivalent of your basic laser. The Concussion Missile is great for taking out Tubbs.

At a Glance

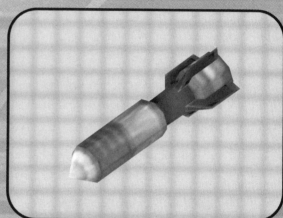

- High-explosive warhead

- Most basic of missiles

- Delivers bruising effects

Frag Missile

Frags provide another deadly punch in the missile arsenal of shrapnel fury. Basically, the Frag Missile is a Concussion Missile with a larger "splash" damage radius.

At a Glance

- Chaotic frag paths make mince-meat out of targets lurking behind corners

- Plenty of boom for the buck

Homing Missile

One of the most reliable of all *Descent 3* missiles, Homing Missiles utilize state-of-the-art tracking systems to ensure hits of all kinds. This weapon is great for the less than average pilots.

At a Glance

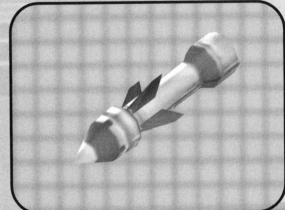

- Infrared targeting

- Great for tackling agile foes, including Orbots and Squids

- The dogfighter's weapon of choice

Guided Missile

Guided Missiles, with their remote-piloting flight control, make all difficult to reach targets accessible. On the other hand, these missiles are very quick, so learning to pilot them can take some practice.

At a Glance

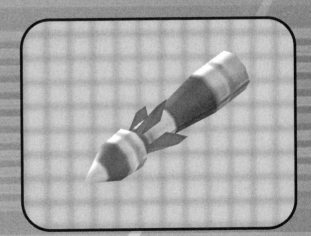

- Top-of-the-line system eradicates those annoying, hard to reach Bots

- Capable of being steered around numerous corners and long distances

- Challenging to fly

Impact Mortar

When you're looking for a dramatic finish, drop an Impact Mortar down the chute. This is a very slow munition that causes major damage. This is the weapon of choice for clearing a room of unsuspecting Bots.

At a Glance

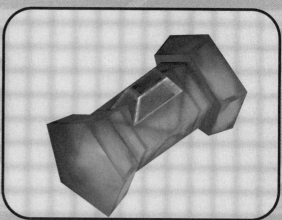

- Gravity-propelled, high-explosive device

- Blasts apart hard to open places

- Blasts apart hard to reach Bots

Napalm Rocket

If you could package the Napalm Cannon into missile form, it would take the form of the Napalm Rocket. This weapon has all the advantages of the Napalm Cannon, plus it has range.

At a Glance

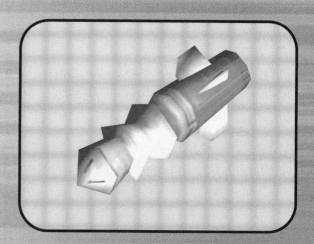

- Intense torching power

- Throws blobs of flaming Napalm everywhere when launched into a ceiling or wall

- Similar to the Napalm Cannon with range

Smart Missile

One of the most "intelligent" rockets on the market, the Smart Missile makes gunning down targets incredibly easy. The Smart Missile is similar to the Guided Missile on steroids.

At a Glance

- Save these for the really tough fights

- Explodes in a frenzy of green plasma projectiles

- Divides upon impact, striking the nearest target

Cyclone Missile

The hounds of hell have a new name—the Cyclone Missile. The ultimate swarm clearer, the Cyclone Missile can dispose of a lot of Bots at once.

At a Glance

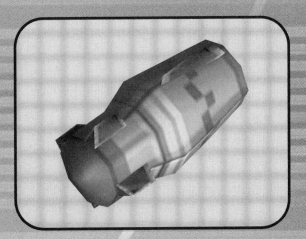

- Features heat-seeking tracking system

- One missile unleashes six mini-missiles

- Don't waste the effects on single foes

Mega Missile

Armed with a conventional explosive warhead, the Mega Missile doesn't mess around when it comes to eradicating enemy Bots from your path. The Mega Missile is similar to the Impact Mortar.

At a Glance

- One of the most powerful projectiles in missile technology

- Can blow away the toughest assault machines with just one or two shots

- Excellent for handling Bosses like Homunculus

Blackshark Missile

The Blackshark Missile can quickly send enemy Bots into oblivion. Like the manual says, "The Blackshark streaks to its target and creates an infinite abyss—from the vortex of the Blackshark Missile there is no retreat."

At a Glance

- Newest and most dangerous of top-secret weapons

- Sucks robots into an infinite abyss of time-space

The Last Weapon

Well, that's your weapon primer. You've mastered basic piloting strategies, studied the bad guys, and memorized the weapons—I guess it's time to start playing. Turn the page to descend into the missions of *Descent 3*.

The Missions

Chapter Four:
The Missions

Ready for some virtual reality vertigo? There are fifteen missions of rip-roaring fun in *Descent 3*, consisting of an interplanetary journey and numerous battles with robot hordes. There are even a couple of hidden missions; but first things first. You need to find Dr. Sweitzer's whereabouts. So hop into your Pyro GL spacecraft, and let's begin the third installment of Descent!

Mission One

We'll drop you off at the P.T.M.C. Crisis Contingency Management and Public Relations Data Retention Center on Deimos.

Find the Data Terminal in the lower level of the facility and use it to download the personnel records into your ship's computer. From these records, we should be able to find the exact location of Dr. Sweitzer.

Once you have the data, head back outside where we'll pick you up.

Objectives

- Deactivate the Containment Force Field
- Find the Main Data Retention Complex
- Get the Restricted Access Pass key
- Access the Mainframe
- Find Data on Sweitzer's location
- Escape the Facility

Enemies

- Gyros
- Orbots
- Tubbs
- Squids

Walkthrough

Head towards the left tunnel, hugging the inside wall, but beware of the two Gyros lurking ahead. Continue nestling the wall, and put your crosshairs on the first Bot. Let him have it. Now prepare to face the second Gyro. You're not gonna catch him off guard like the first one, so prepare for a little competition. After toasting him, collect all the **Shield** and **Energy Power-Ups** in the area.

Locate the two tunnels ahead, and go through the one to your left. As you enter, take the next entrance to your immediate left. Don't be tricked by the steam and the red lights; you are a far cry from some cosmic nightclub. Be advised that danger lurks ahead. In fact, an Orbot is hovering in the chamber, hiding amidst the haze. Remain on the outside of that area, and take it out.

Tip

In general, don't head into the location of the steam duct without first blotting out the Orbot. First, saunas aren't allowed. Second, the mist will only cloud your perception, enabling the Orbot to knock out your lights before you know what hits you. Of course, if it flees and doesn't return after a moment or two, go in after it.

Make your way to the end of the tunnel. Two doors will appear, one on the bottom and one on the top. Enter the bottom door, but beware of the two Gyros to your right. Weave in and out, using the portal area as a shield. After eradicating these baddies, collect the **Power-Ups** in the area and head down the shaft.

Mission One

There's a door to your left at the end of the tunnel. Further to your right is a force-shielded exit that leads outside. For the sake of quickness, grab the **Concussion Missile** near the right exit, and then take the left door. As you enter, navigate up to reach another door above the one you just entered. The containment switch is located here, the one with yellow and black markings. Shoot the device  with your lasers to deactivate the force field below. Go back down to the corridor with the force-shielded exit. Head out the newly opened passage, making way for the Data Retention Complex.

Fly through the Deimos landscape, moving forward in a fairly straight path. The valley you traverse is crooked, but it doesn't cut right or left. Notice the structure ahead with the turret above the entrance? That is the Data Retention Complex.

Note

Watch out for the wandering Bots and the turrets. A turret also rests on the structure adjacent to the Data Retention Complex entrance. This means that you must dodge two firing turrets on your way inside, as well as some menacing Bots. Don't waste your time out here; hurry up and get inside!

While dodging the barrage of fire, rush in and scoop up the **Concussion Missile** located near the entrance. Hurry through the tunnel, because the turret can still hit you from this point. Watch out for the Gyros, Orbots, and a Tubbs. Be cautious, creeping into each angle of the tunnel as you head down, and watch out for the charging Tubbs. Although it doesn't have any weapons, its punch is fairly devastating.

Tubbs can be a real pain. It will lunge at you in a heartbeat, even while you're firing at it! The best thing to do is back up. This gives you more room to blast the overzealous bully. Although it will take several shots with the laser, it will usually only take one or two with a Concussion Missile.

A lot of Bots will try to deter your movement up the shaft. Unfortunately, the tunnel is rather lengthy; however, there is some good news. An Energy Center, the room with a golden glow, is located to the left. The combat thus far may have damaged your shields, so head inside the yellow markings to recharge them if they are less than 100. When you're finished, head for a small intermediate chamber (purple in color). Look to your right for **Four Concussion Missiles** (one pack), but be wary of any patrolling Gyros.

After grabbing the missile pack, continue to slip down the shaft. There's a large room with four windows at the tunnel's end. After gunning down the Orbot, send a Concussion Missile through the windows. After doing so, take out the Gyros, enter the room, and collect the **Power-Ups**. Now levitate towards the top windows and put a Concussion Missile through one of them.

Go through the broken window, turn right, and head for the tunnel entrance. Oftentimes, there's a couple of Gyros there to greet you. Continue through this shaft until you reach a "C-shaped" room. After disposing of the Gyros, collect the **Power-Ups**. The chamber has several of these; one is located in front of the left door. Take that exit.

Mission One

When the tunnel forks, take the right path. This area is heavily guarded by Orbots, so be prepared. Enter the first door on the left, but note that several Gyros await behind the portal. Shred some tin and collect the **Power-Ups** and **Concussion Missile Pack**. Drift downward until you locate the **Restricted Access Passkey** near the Mainframe. Next, access the terminal by first bumping into it. Then, when prompted, press the *F8* and *Shift keys* to download the information. Press the same keys again to remove the information from your visor.

Note

The Mainframe reports that a recent SRAB Lab accident is responsible for the deaths of 17 scientists. Samuel Dravis, the Director of Crisis Contingency Management & Public Relations, has terminated Dr. Karl Sweitzer's employment as a result of the incident.

You're almost finished! You need to find the second terminal, and it's not in this room. Leave the chamber and head to the left. Locate the next door on the left. After mopping them up with some Concussion Missiles, head inside. Prepare to take down some Gyros. Slip down towards the terminal, but watch out for a Squid to your left. One Concussion Missile should finish it off. Bump into the terminal and press *F8* and *Shift* to access the data.

The data recovered reveals that Sweitzer is serving time at Novak Corporate Prison on Phobos. When you finish accessing the terminal, press *Shift* and *F8*, and then head up the same way you came. Three ducts lie across the room's exit. Behind one of them is a four-missile pack of **Homing Missiles**. Now head to the left from the room's exit, looking for an exit covered with a blue grate. Blast the alloy lattice with a Concussion Missile. Presto! Escape to the safety from the cleared orifice.

Mission One

Mission Two

The data shows that Dr. Sweitzer is currently at Novak on Phobos. He was sent there by order of Samuel Dravis. We'll drop you off just outside an old maintenance tunnel. From there you'll need to make your way to the main tower, create a diversion, and find Sweitzer. Once you have him, we'll send a shuttle to get him to safety.

Objectives

- Eliminate perimeter defenses
- Destroy all prison records' databanks
- Rescue Dr. Sweitzer

Enemies

- Thiefbot
- Squid
- Gyro
- Tubbs
- Orbot

Walkthrough

The door behind you is locked. As you fly through the caverns, you'll meet a Orbot and recover a four-pack of **Concussion Missiles**. Eventually, you'll see a grate adjacent to a Novak sign. Blow out the grate and enter the complex.

There's a Bot down the first tunnel to the right. Kill it and swoop into the chamber. Take out the pair of waiting Gyros, and pick up the four-pack of **Homing Missiles**. Now return to the main tunnel and hang a right.

There's a connecting shaft in the ceiling near the end of the main tunnel. Follow the shaft into a large room with two Tubbs. Eliminate them, and escape out the door.

Note

There are three boxes in a corner of the room. Destroy them to get one Energy and one Shield Power Up.

Exit the building, turn around, and collect the **Energy** and **Shield Power-Ups**. Watch out for an incoming Gyro, take it out, and circle the mountain in front of you. En route you'll find five fixed laser platforms. Take one out and the shuttle will hail you. Eliminate the other four and you'll get the go-ahead to enter the Supply Depot.

Mission Two

Note

Move in a clockwise position around the canyon, destroying each laser in turn. The Supply Depot is within sight of the final tower.

There are some Tubbs and Gyros waiting in the Depot. Vaporize the welcoming party, and then pick up the **Rapid Fire Power-Up** in the alcove in the entranceway ceiling. Enter the main room next. There's a **Security Pass** in the back of the room, a **Guided Missile** in the room above the entrance (watch out for the Tubbs), and a trio of **Homing Missiles** in the "attic."

Collect all the **Power-Ups**, and then plunge into the caverns below. The first room has a Tubbs, Gyros, Squid, and assorted other Bots. After disposing of them, pick up the **Power-Ups** (there are also **Quad-Lasers** and a couple of **Concussion Missiles** hanging about) and head into the jagged tunnel marked by the lighter-colored rocks.

Tip

Don't dive too low in your dogfights with the Squid. The floor is coated with acid, so coming in contact with it weakens your shields.

Follow the tunnel, waxing the Bots along the way, until you reach a "Y-shaped" part of the tunnel. Take the right path and continue until you find a larger cavern with two large, open pipes. The upper pipe is tempting, but ignore it for now and sweep into the lower tunnel.

Note

Once again, watch out for the acid. A little bit of afterburner goes a long way here!

Follow this tunnel (careful, there's a Squid in there) and exit through the side into another room. Enter the adjacent tunnel, and pick up a couple of the goodies adjacent to the dead-end grill. Return to the room and exit through the hatch.

The next room has a Tubbs in it, so axe it and zip into the back to snap up the **R-1 Security Pass**. There are two exits in this room. Take the one on the same wall as the Security Pass.

Duck down into each of the three pipes, and gather the goodies. Exit through the hatch at the far end of the room. Use the G-1 Security Pass at the check station to gain access to the minimum-security level. Continue through the tunnel until you enter the medium-security ring.

Note

The security "rings" are color-coded. Green indicates minimum, yellow means medium, while red indicates maximum.

Continue to the left through the minimum-security ring until you find a door on your left across from a Bot Generator. Enter the door and feed the Y-1 Security Pass to the station.

Mission Two

Continue down the hall into a square-like tunnel. Above is the Prisoner Transfer Bay, but avoid that area for now. Below is the yellow-streaked entry into medium security. Drop a marker and enter the tunnel. Continue to the medium-security ring, and then hang a right.

Tip

This ring is tougher than the last one. All the guards are Tubbs, so when they appear back away and quickly pump Laser rounds and Concussion Missiles into them.

Fly along the ring until you pass a Bot Generator on the right. The first left is the entrance to maximum security, so enter it and use the R-1 Security Pass at the station. Before moving on, you must find Sweitzer in the maximum-security level. The transport pilot then congratulates you, and asks that you move Sweitzer to the minimum-security level. Here's how.

Follow the entrance tunnel to another square-like, vertical tunnel. Drop down and enter the maximum-security tunnel—note the red stripes.

Note

There's a Squid and a pack of Concussion Missiles below (in the bottom of the square-like tunnel). The Squid is guarding a switch. You'll trip that switch later, but for now destroy the Squid, snap up the missiles, and drop a marker.

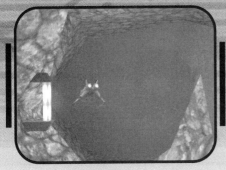

Take a right in the maximum-security ring, and watch out for Squids as you fly through the tunnel. Look for a grated opening on the left; vaporize the guardian Squid and destroy the grate.

Enter the space, take a quick right, and follow the shaft to the top. Plunge into the connecting tunnel and blow out the grate and the Bot at the end. Enter the room and waste the Squid on the left-hand side of the room.

Now comes the fun part! Trip the left switch (by shooting it). When the attending robot gathers the chemicals and moves over the vat, trip the right switch.

The contamination forces the evacuation of the maximum-security level. Accordingly, you know the good doctor is now on his way to the minimum level (i.e. where the shuttle wanted him in the first place).

Unfortunately, the shuttle calls in with a problem: The guy can't get into the prison because of a force field. Rush back to the aforementioned switch room (the one that held the now-eliminated Squid and the Concussion Missile four-pack). Sail out the side openings to reach the top of the tower. Take down the laser turret, and fly through one of the four pipers into the tower room. Fly into the bay and trigger the . wall switch to lower the force fields.

Mission Two

Mission Three

Sweitzer has agreed to help us. He is positive that Davis illegally ordered modifications to the alien virus without approval. We know that Dravis sabotaged your ship to get you out of the way. Sweitzer also believes that Dravis sabotaged his lab to keep him from interfering. When he survived, he was sent to prison.

A backup copy of the work was kept in the bottom of the lab. We must stop Dravis by showing the proof to the president of the P.T.M.C.

Objective

- Recover the data from Sweitzer's lab on Tiris.

Enemies

- Thiefbot
- Squid
- Gyro
- Tubbs
- Orbot
- Stinger

Walkthrough

They've locked the door behind you, so there is no turning back. Near your initial drop point you'll find **Missiles** and a frag. For more extras, fire at the boxes on the floor and pick up the **Power-Ups**. Leave the area through the door directly across from the docking bay.

As you travel though the tunnel, you will come across some Orbots. Enter the circular room with some caution, because there are a number of Squids, Orbots and Tubbs.

As you go around the middle pillar, beware of a Tubbs and an Orbot. Continue to the door on the other side of the room. Upon entering the door, you're greeted by more Bots.

You should now be on Level One. Proceed up into the tube to access Level Two. Go down the hallway and continue through the doorway. As you enter the doorway, prepare to battle some Squids.

Note

There are two turrets on the floor below the gangway on the right and the left. They are guarding a switch under the floor.

After turning the switch, go back onto the gangway. Now face the control panel and enter the tube on the left. Use caution, though, because even though there's plenty of loot, it's being guarded by some overzealous bad guys. Also, make sure you blow up the boxes for extra shields and energy.

Exit the tube the way you entered it, and continue past the control panel and through the door. (Watch out for the ceiling turret.) Pass through this area (there is a tunnel on your right that is blocked by a force field), and proceed straight ahead to the next doorway. Upon entering that chamber, note the Squid on the right and Tubbs to the left.

Mission Three

Note

To deactivate the force field, you must flip the switch.

Now go back and enter the tunnel that was previously blocked by the force field.

Stop at the edge of the tunnel leading to the outside. Shoot the circuit-like area on each of the four towers between the bottom square and the spike (the one that resembles a pencil).

After accomplishing this task, wait for lightning to overload and destroy the tower, which will deactivate the force field of the tunnel directly across from your position.

Enter the tunnel, fly to the door marked "Level Three," and enter hallway. Swoop into the hallway on the left, and then take another left. This hallway expands into a large round room with a turret on the ceiling.

Note

If you hit the opposite wall, it will open to reveal a Secret Room that contains Invulnerability.

The door on the right is locked. Enter the hallway on the left and head toward the force field. At this point, you'll enter a large room with two hallways. Enter the hallway on the right and activate the switch behind the pillar to engage the Primary Coupling. Go back and do the same thing in the room directly across.

Note

Activating these switches diverts the Auxiliary Power to the Datalink System.

Leave this area through the large room, and return to where the door was previously locked. Enter the room and arrange the switches.

Note

Arrange the levers in the correct sequence to complete the Datalink. The sequence follows: second to left goes down, the remainder go up. You have just activated the Datalink Communication Transmission. Now you have access to the Armory.

Return to the room where the force field once was, and scoop up all the unprotected loot.

Leave this area, proceed straight ahead, and enter the tunnel on the right. Follow the tunnel until it ends, turn, and enter the tunnel on the right. Then, when it ends (there will be a red PTMC sign in front of you), turn to the left. Follow the hallway door. Enter the door and head up past the Level Three sign.

Enter the hallway below the sign and follow it until it ends (the door facing you is locked). Turn to the right, and follow the long hallway until it empties into a round room. Open the door on the right. Follow the hallway until it spills into a rectangular room, and then clear the room and pick up the **Security Key**. Retrace your steps, and use the Security Key to open the previously locked door.

Follow the hallway as it twists and turns. Turn on your craft's headlights and dive into the caves. Follow the caves around to the left until you reach a blocked area. Clear out the rocks with a Frag Missile and exit the caves.

Mission Three

Watch the ground for a patrol as you leave the caves. There are two turrets mounted on the roof of the building. Follow the road that leads away from the building. Go to the left (behind the broken down building), and enter the mouth of the ruins with the blue glowing eyes.

Head down toward the lava. Stay parallel to the molten metal until you reach the opposite side of the ruins. When you reach the end, go up above the blue stone and exit the ruins through the opening. Blow out the windows of the building on the left.

After enter the building, head straight down into a round room with four doors. Only two of the doors have switches (the switches allow you to manually lock and unlock the doors).

Note

Watch out for the Thiefbot. It will steal whatever it can get its hands on. You'll need to shoot it repeatedly to get back any stolen goods as well as the data cartridge.

Head through the door over the broken walkway, and take a right at the intersection. Through the second door you'll find the Thiefbot, who has stolen the data cartridge. Destroy it and retrieve the data cartridge when it drops it.

Return to the central area and head through the door across from the broken floor. Take a left at the intersection and pass through another door. In this large room you'll find the upload nodes to your right. Place the cartridge between the nodes by using the "\" key.

Note

Exit through the opposite end of the upload node room.

Activate the door and turn to the right. Next, activate the switch to upload the data. Now sit back and watch the animation window as the Super Thief steals the cartridge. Return to the previous room where the upload nodes are located.

Note

Use the manual locks on the doors to trap the SuperThief in an area you find most comforting.

To recapture the cartridge, you must dispose of this Bot. With the cartridge in your possession, leave this area and return to the central area. Head straight up and out of the building to end the mission.

Mission Four

We thought you'd like to take the evidence to Suzuki yourself. We'll get you to Seoul. Your fighter craft may be viewed as hostile, so we'll drop you off in the subway. Watch out for the Police Bots protecting the city.

Fly to the P.T.M.C. Tower and deliver the evidence. Make sure you return to the Red Acropolis afterwards so we can hear what happened!

Objectives

- Get to the train station
- Find the entrance to the sewers
- Find the P.T.M.C. Tower
- Upload the data to Suzuki

Enemies

- Old Scratch
- Gyro
- Thiefbot
- Tailbot
- Tubbs
- Squid
- Orbot
- Black Pyro

Walkthrough

You're finally back on Earth, but this mission is not going to be easy. In fact, I hope you're not claustrophobic or scared of the dark, because you begin this mission in the subways of Seoul, Korea. The subway system is dark and dank, plus a few Scratches lurk below too. However, you have a job to do, so crawl into your ship and turn on the headlights!

Note

The Automap is a definite necessity in this mission. Without it, you won't be able to see where you're going. Don't be afraid to use it.

You begin this mission in a subway tunnel that does not have access to trains. In fact, the shaft leads to dead ends on both sides. Collect the **Afterburner Cooler**, and then slip through the opening to the left.

Note

Don't venture out too soon, because these tunnels have a busy schedule. The subway trains are always on the run, and if they hit you, you're a goner!

Tip

Study the train pattern. In general, the best time to launch your ship onto the subway tunnels is right after two trains pass by. In particular, when the second train follows the tail end of the first train.

Mission Four

Zoom to the left and land on the first sidewell. Position your craft on the very last compartment of this well, and then launch onto the second sidewell. Now launch from the last compartment on this well onto another opening to your right (similar to the first one you saw in the first shaft).

After studying the train pattern again, head to the right to the next sidewell. This time you must use your Afterburner to make it. Do the same to reach the second sidewell. From this point, you must find the opening to your left.

Tip

Scratches make appearances in various sidewells and openings. Don't worry though, because only one Scratch will attack at a time. Resist the temptation to venture onto (or near) the tracks to engage these creeps. In short, do the best you can within the cramped quarters.

Head to the left from this opening to reach another sidewell. You'll need special timing and the use of Afterburner to succeed. Look for an opening to your right after landing on the second sidewell. You're almost out of the subway system!

The Train Station should be to your right. It's a lengthier haul to this area than to most of the other spots on the subway. Again, using Afterburner and superior timing, head to the right, down the left side of the tracks. The Station should be just ahead and to your left.

This completes your first objective, reaching the Train Station. With this task finished, head up to the city streets. "Freeze." Ignore the Gyros' warning, and instead mop them up. Grab the **Power-Ups** and **Concussion Missile Pack**. Up ahead near the intersection, keep a watchful eye out for a Tubbs and Tailbot.

After hanging a right, you'll reach a corner that heads to the left. There's also another street nearby to your right; however, it's a dead end road. Watch out for a Stinger and Tubbs on an ambush. Teach these pests a lesson in hospitality, and then continue straight.

Note

Watch out for the Bots patrolling the streets. Now you know why you must find your way to the P.T.M.C. Tower from within the subway and sewer systems.

Another corner is ahead, so when you reach it head to the left. Also, there are some **Homing Missiles** stashed inside a cubbyhole to the left along the walls with the Oriental posters. As you're stocking up, keep your eyes peeled. A Squid and Tubbs will try to ambush you here, plus the Thiefbot may make an appearance.

This road has an Energy Center to the left, next to the branching to the left. After you collect the **Concussion Missile Pack,** go inside the Enery Center to recharge. Upon entering, an unruly gang of Bots (Tubbs, Gyros, and Stingers) will charge you. Brush them off, using the Energy Center as a barrier of sorts.

Mission Four

Note

The Napalm Gun and Concussion Missiles near the Energy Center are an excellent aid in taking out this Bot gang.

Go straight ahead until you reach the first right, which you need to take. This path zigzags at several points, and there are some goodies stashed inside the cubbyholes along the walls. At the end of this street you'll see a rusty street grate. Blast the grate with a missile and then enter.

Tip

Two Stingers will try to dispose of you as you enter the grate. Take them out from above; if you don't, they will follow you into the sewer. To get through the sewer, do the following: left, left, right, left, straight.

As you descend further, you'll face more Squids and a Stinger. Head to the right, and then take a quick left at the intersection. Axe the green Squids and Stingers. When you reach an intersection, hang a right. After disposing of the Stinger, take the first left.

At the next intersection, proceed straight ahead. There's a shaft in the ceiling towards the end of this tunnel. This shaft leads outside, near the P.T.M.C. building. Ascend up the shaft to a Neon sign hanging on the wall.

When you arrive at street level, head down the street to the only street-level door. Go through it and the one immediately after it. The P.T.M.C. Tower is directly ahead.

Tip

The Black Pyros primarily shoot Super Lasers. You can send them spiraling with some Homing and Concussion Missiles.

Progress towards the big gray door below the tower. Fly to the center of the nodes and upload the Data Cartridge. (Select your Data Cartridge from your inventory, and then press "/".) Retrace your steps. Two P.T.M.C. Mercenaries will greet you in Black Pyros. To finish the job, simply dispose of these baddies.

Mission Four

Mission Five

There is no official briefing for Mission Five. Instead, sit back, relax and watch the FMV that pops up between the completion of Mission Four and Mission Five.

Objectives

- Keep 3 out of the 5 Reactors operational
- Escape from Red Acropolis

Enemies

- Squid
- Stinger
- Flametrooper

Walkthrough

The level begins just as you arrive at your Pyro in the hangar. You need to keep three of the five reactors online for the evacuation of Red Acropolis to continue safely. After 12 minutes of keeping them online, return to the second main hangar room and exit through the door in the ceiling.

In the initial hangar below the deck, there are a bunch of **Power-ups**, so collect them before you go through the door you're initially facing. Collect the **Green Map** near the first pillar across from the entrance. Also, note that the far right wall has been broken. A stream of Squids will slowly pour out, but don't waste your ammo on them. Fight off the Red Stormtrooper as he tries to burn you to death.

Tip

Below the first main area is a long shaft leading to a room with a couple of Stingers and plenty of Power-ups. If you're lacking firepower at the beginning of the level, head down there to find a Plasma and other weapons, but you don't need to destroy the Stingers.

Head through Door #1 after collecting more **Power-ups** from the main hub. Follow the passageway to the end, and destroy the Stingers first, because they can cause damage quickly. After they're gone, destroy all the Squids in the reactor room. Again, collect all **Power-ups** as you do this, especially since the Bots will mostly be focused on firing at the reactor. Once Reactor Room 1 is clear, head back towards the main hub, but take a left at the rotating light.

Destroy any Squids and Stormtroopers as you encounter them. You'll pass through a door and come to a room where there's been another breach of Red Acropolis. Destroy all of the lurking Bots and collect the **Gunboys**. Head down through the door on the floor. When you reach the bottom door at the end the long vertical tube,

Mission Five

drop all of your **Gunboys** just before the door in a little group while facing down. This will enable them to damage any invaders coming down the tube. Continue through the door.

Collect the **Rapid Fire** and go through the door below the warning light. This takes you to Reactor Room 2, where you'll need to eliminate the Bots as quickly as possible.

Note

Fight the Squids from the side if at all possible. They'll get distracted by the reactors, and you'll avoid getting hit by the attacking forces' shots.

Now take a good look at the reactor display on the left side of the screen. Because you only need to keep 3 reactors operational, you must choose to defend between Reactor 3 and Reactor 4 in addition to Reactors 1 and 2. If Reactor 3 has more shields remaining than Reactor 4, defend it. If Reactor 4 has more remaining, you should defend 4 instead. If both reactors are near the same level, choose Reactor 3 and follow along, because we'll assume it is your third reactor for the rest of the level.

Note

Always know the quickest way to the main hub, because you'll be using it to run between the reactor areas.

Head back out of Reactor Room 2. When you reach the room with the second breach, go through the door across from it. Always destroy any Squids you see from this point forward. When you reach the main hub, head to the left through Door 3. Follow the winding tunnel around. When you reach a vertical shaft, collect the **Homing Missiles** and head down.

Homing Missiles are your friends in this mission. Collect and use them to finish off any particularly dodgy Bots. You don't have time to wear down one robot for a minute or two.

There's a slightly rippling wall at the bottom of those shafts. It's just an illusion, so go right through it and pick up the **Cloak** below. Go through the bottom of the two doors at the end of the shaft and follow another winding tunnel.

When attacking Bots in the reactor rooms, you must be careful of where you shoot because your weapons can damage the reactor. The Lasers are the least destructive, so you can fire at enemies near the reactor. However, it's best to only fire missiles when the Bots are some distance from the reactor. Missiles can be very destructive!

This takes you to Reactor 3. Clear the room of attackers, collect the **Power-ups**, and get out quickly (use the same way you came in). On your way back, head into the second to bottom door, destroy the Stinger, and make a quick round of the energy center. The four Gunboys will come in handy, blocking the path of invading robots.

Mission Five

Tip

Don't worry about Reactors 4 and 5. Remember that the mission is to keep 3 out of 5 reactors online, and there is no bonus for keeping all five online.

When you return to the main hub, take another glance at the reactor status display. Reactors 1, 2, and 3 are your only concern, so get back to 1 or 2 and fight off the new invaders.

From this point on, you must perform a balancing act between those three reactors. Keep them operational for the remainder of the 12 minutes, rushing between them to fight off new invaders. Use Gunboys and every other weapon you can find to destroy Squids whenever you see them. If Reactor 3 is relatively safe, focus your efforts on destroying the Bots as they're generated between Reactors 1 and 2.

For more **Power-ups**, head down toward Reactor 5. After the door in the ceiling, head straight over a ridge toward a door. Just past the door is a room with a pillar and a group of **Power-ups**. You'll find an **Invulnerability** and **Rapid Fire** as well as more missiles.

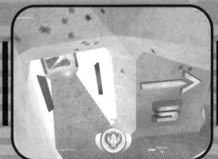

Once the 12 minutes expire, again head back to the main hub, and exit the level through the door above the hangar entrance. You'll only have 90 seconds to escape, so get there as quickly as you can! Take a look as you fly out, and watch and see Red Acropolis go down in flames.

Mission Five

Mission Six

During our escape, a C.E.D. Interceptor crash-landed in an isolated region of Mars. Before you head back to the Beagle, you should locate it. We'll need all the resources we can get.

Mutants who occupy this area have taken the ship underground. Fly through the canyons and force your way in through the Nomads' loading platform. A tug ship will wait on the surface during your mission, and will assist you once you've located the ship.

Objectives

- Find the crashed C.E.D. ship
- Enter the nomad caverns
- Find the Collector's Icon
- Find the Builder's Icon
- Use the icons
- Find the Priest's Icon
- Use the Priest's Icon

Enemies

- Seeker
- Pest
- Old Scratch
- Tailbot
- Orbot

Walkthrough

You're on Mars. Navigate your ship through the canyon, being careful not to brush up against the sides. Eventually, a loading platform (with two long towers) will appear to your left. First, take out the Nomad-powered UFO machines using your Lasers, and then do the same with the two Seekers patrolling the area. The Seekers will inform everyone that you're here.

After cleaning up the canyon, shoot at the base of the two towers. Two or three shots with the Lasers at each spot (the black part with red lights) will drop the hatch. Now descend into the infernal regions, but beware of a nest of Pests resting on the ceiling. You should eliminate them before they eliminate you. Descend another level lower to blot out the three Old Scratches; otherwise, these guys will attack you later.

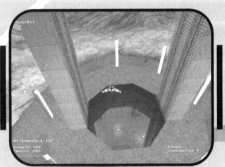

Note **Small, cloaked figures with scepters roam the floor. These are the Nomads. Although they are known for their bizarre rituals and strange beliefs, these mutants will not cause you any harm unless manning a craft.**

Proceed back to the first level (the one where the Pests were located). Go to the pit in front of you and grab the pack of **Homing Missiles**. (Believe me, these will come in handy down here!) There are two doorways here: one on your far right and one on your far left. The left portal leads to the **Builder Icon**, while the right portal leads to the **Collector Icon**.

Fire into the left entrance, but don't enter because an Orbot, Scratch, and several Pests are in that room. Try to dispose of them from outside the portal, using Homing Missiles and Lasers. You'll need to dodge some fire, but that will be much easier than using the portal as a shield and barrier.

Mission Six

Be very careful upon entering the left door marked with the Builder Icon sign. A Pest and Orbot are located directly over the door. Try to lure them out before entering.

Collect the **Napalm Fuel** and **Power-Ups** in the dark, closet-like area to your right, but don't forget the **Concussion Missile** to your left. Continue down the corridor, wary of the two Pests hanging on the wall. After eliminating them, prepare for a little monster mash. Several Tailbots, Pests, and an Orbot are in the room with the caldron. Use your Laser and Homing Missiles on these guys. Collect the **Vauss**, **Power-Ups**, **Napalm Fuel**, **Impact Mortar**, **Vauss Rounds**, and **Concussion Missiles** stashed within the various nooks and crannies of the room

Note

There's a Super Laser hidden in the shaft near the lava pit.

Continue down the corridor, blasting the Orbots, Tailbots, Pests, and Old Scratch before collecting the goodies. Head into the next room, the one with the caldron. Finish off the Pests and Orbots, and then collect the **Napalm Gun**, **Power-Ups** (there's also one for the Guide Bot), **Missiles**, and **Seeker Mines**.

Tip

The Pests are appropriately named! These things love to hang on ceiling columns and over entrances. So before entering a room, look all around to make sure the room is clear.

Fly over the caldron, and then slowly navigate up. This shaft leads to an outside area where you will face your first puzzle. Take out the Nomad fighter crafts, and then try to solve the puzzle, which involves those big, wrench-like structures. Fly through the first structure without a reddish-speckled cover, and continue to navigate through each (just like threading a needle) as each cover disappears. The eighth one contains the icon; just fly into it to collect it.

Before returning, collect all of the goodies outside. (For example, there's a pack of **Vauss Rounds** near the foot of the stone.) Go back via the opening in the boulder. Leave the room with the caldron and return to the one with the lava pit.

Take the door to your left, but be advised that this area is heavily protected. Try to take out as many critters as possible from the portal. Once the area is clean, collect the **Power-Ups**, **Missiles**, **Mines**, and other goodies. Find the sign with the Builder Icon. It's on the wall (near the top), just above the steel beams on the floor.

Head to the lobby where all the Nomads are gathered. Enter the right door, staying near the portal. Fire into the open to make some Nomad fighting machines and Scratches appear. The area to your right is infested with Old Scratches, while the area straight ahead is crawling with Pests. After eliminating the Bots, pick up the hidden goodies in these two rooms, including a **Homing Missile** near the lava pit.

See the door ahead? "Knock" on it with your Laser. Two Pests should be in the entrance, so blast them to pieces. The area you're now in looks like a mineshaft. Take the **Homing Missile** near the corridor ceiling, above the shaft strips. At this point, the shaft branches out and, to make matters worse, this place is heavily infested with Tailbots and Scratches. Take out as many as possible before advancing.

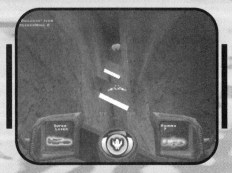

Head towards the right, smoking as many critters as possible. Ascend to where the elevated path (tan plated tiles) begins on your right. The **Collector Icon** is hovering in this crevice, just above the light strips. You'll probably need to turn around to see it. After grabbing it, continue down the path.

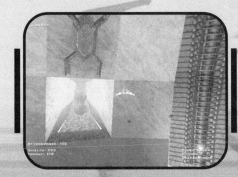

The path leads to another room, one that contains a door with a circular lock. Collect the **Vauss Rounds** and **Concussion Missiles** near it. Enter the door, which will now open because you have the Builder Icon. Locate the three Icon signs near the ceiling. Place the Builder Icon in the purple vault under its respective icon. You can do this by sorting through your inventory, and then placing it by using the "/" key. Do the same for the Collector Icon.

Enter the door, which will now open because the Icons have been placed. This place is crawling with Bots, so it's best to dispose of them from afar. Beware of the Scratches though; they love to sneak up on you from under the platform. Finish it off by taking out the Tailbots in the purple domed area. Next, enter the door with the **Priest Icon** above it (it's directly under the door from which you entered).

Note

The room with the Priest Icon is filled with golden columns. You are told that the "chosen one" walks around in this room. Don't go looking for him or her. The "chosen one" is you —that is if you play your cards right.

The trick is in the ceiling tiles. Look at each tile. There are arrows above to guide you to the Icon. Notice the light-colored, "V-shaped" panels in each of the "Xs" on the ceiling? These are arrows. Go the direction that each arrow indicates. Some ceiling tiles that you pass over do not have arrows. Continue going in the direction that the previous tile's arrow indicated. You will come to one tile near the shielded altar of the Icon. It contains a light-colored "X." First, head to the left and continue going where the arrows indicate. Finally, you will return to the same tile with the light-colored "X." Move towards the tile to its right. "You are worthy!" The Icon is now attainable.

Grab the Priest Icon. Leave the multi-pillared chamber and head for the dome-like structure in the other room. Place the Icon in the purple vault (it resembles the vaults for the Builder and Collector Icons). Take the opposing door (it's in the domed area). Dispose of the Nomad UFO and Orbot near the entrance, and collect the **Impact Mortar** near the top right-hand part of the room.

Enter through the large tunnel ahead, noting that some Seekers and other Bots are in the next room. Watch your back for the two Nomad UFOs and the Orbot; they will sneak up on you. Clean up this bunch, and then gobble up the **Power-Ups**. You're about finished, but first you must take on Homunculus. Head down the blue force-fielded tube. Your destiny awaits you!

Homunculus is one bad son-of-a-gun. Its lair is small, but there is plenty of room to dismantle this beast. Collect the **Missiles** near the back part of the lair, and shoot Homunculus with everything you have. It's even better when you shoot the Lasers with a round from one of the other available weapons (Mortars, Homing Missiles, and Concussions) at the same time.

Tip

Shoot and move is the name of the game here. Always jostle around, rising to the ceiling as often as possible, watching out for Homunculus' fireball. Its important to constantly shoot at this monster to wear it down. By doing so, you will prevent it from rejuvenating its shields, which is the only way to defeat Homunculus.

You will find the lost C.E.D. Interceptor in Homunculus' lair. Once you toast him, your mission is complete.

Mission Six

Mission Seven

The C.E.D. remain unaware of Dravis' virus experiments. Our scientists have started work on an anti-virus to combat his efforts. Our data, however, is quite old and we need to obtain a current sample.

A P.T.M.C. mine on Ceres has recently been revamped, and we show a new magnetic signature well below the surface. Dr. Sweitzer believes that this is where we should look.

Objectives

- Disable surface defenses
- Enable descending accelerator
- Get Security Key
- Disable containment force fields
- Collect both virus samples

Enemies

- Sparky
- Gunslinger
- Squid
- Old Scratch
- Gyro
- Orbot
- Tubbs

Walkthrough

Your ship is hovering above a metallic brown structure. Collect the **Homing Missiles**, **Quad Lasers**, **Afterburner Cooler**, and **Super Laser** near the bottom of the edifice. Head forward and then turn left when you spot a building ahead. If the terrain permits, keep moving left until you're almost in the opposite direction from which you started.

Watch out for the turrets while navigating the surface of Ceres. Because it's difficult to take them out, your best bet is to avoid them whenever possible.

Find a structure with eight entrances. (It's the only building with more than two openings.) Beware of the turrets firing from two sides of the edifice, and enter from one of the other sides to avoid getting hit.

When inside, collect all of the goodies (a **Napalm Gun** and an **Invulnerability Power-Up** among others). Hit the four switches (near the ceiling) with your Laser. This action will activate a blue column within the center of the chamber. To disable the system defenses, shoot the blue column. Now you can enter the P.T.M.C. mine.

Note

Some of the turrets on the Cerean structures will be deactivated, but not all of them.

Collect the **Frag Missile Packs** and **Power-Ups** in some of the small, nearby structures. Then proceed to the nearest structure with a single opening. This structure is rather tall. Upon entering, be careful of the two floating Sparkys. Gun them down, and head below. Next, enter the gray-colored, cave-like section. After you dispose of the two Gryos, proceed through the door marked "P.T.M.C." This is the mine that contains the magnetic signature.

Enter the room cautiously, because there's a horde of Gyros and Stingers awaiting. You can smoke them with your Super Laser and Homing Missiles. Collect all the goodies in the process too. However, before you leave, dismantle the coolant system. To do so, shoot out the blue squares to your left.

Note

The coolant system involves the large, icy blue structures to your left. Dismantling these structures can buy you some precious time needed to collect the virus.

Go through the door and blast the two Gyros. Make sure, however, that you first shoot out the turret attached to the ceiling. After doing so, proceed straight. There are two entrances ahead: a large one that dips below, and a small one almost directly across. Take the small one, in the upper portal.

Turn to your right and take this tunnel to an Energy Center. First, take out the Sparkys and Stingers, but also be aware of the Squids that will ambush from behind. Don't worry about disposing of them, unless it becomes necessary. When the right passage is clear, make a run for it.

There's an Energy Center to your left, and after numerous Bot battles, you'll probably need some extra juice to keep going. In fact, go there and recharge if your Energy points are less than 100. The Center will boost your numbers back to the century mark.

Tip

While recharging, a Sparky will crash your party. Sizzle his goose and head out.

Continue down that passage, taking out the Stinger and Sparky waiting at the exit. Then hang a left, but watch out for two Orbots and another Sparky. Blast them to pieces, and then go to the next room. This is where the Steam Chamber is located. Hit the switch to release the steam release valve.

Return to the room from which you just left (the one right before the Steam Chamber). Slip down the hole at the bottom of this cavern; below is a glowing pillar. A number of Bots will rush you, including a Squid, Scratch, Sparky, and some Gunslingers. After mopping up these bad guys, take the entrance to your immediate left (the smallest of the two openings). Fly through the tunnel into an amber-colored cavern, and erase the lurking Scratch and Gunslinger in the process.

Descend into the bluish realm, and keep moving until you spot a large orange pillar. There's a Gunslinger twirling its guns above you, oblivious to your whereabouts. Take it out with a couple of Homing Missiles. There are two entrances to this area, so take the one on the bottom. At the end of the path is a room with an amber glow.

Note

There's an Energy Center directly above this shaft. There are also several items stashed in it, so take them. Note that this is the last of the Energy Centers on the mission.

Head to your right, and eliminate Sparky and the Stinger. Now descend to the realm under the blinking light, and then turn around. This marks the location of one of the switches you must deactivate. Shoot the switch, and swing over to the left room. Descend to the realm under the blinking light, but watch out for a Sparky. Blast that baddie, and then hit the switch. While you're there, check underneath the pipe work for some **Power-Ups** and **Frag Missiles**. With the switches deactivated, the door located straight ahead will open.

Do not enter the room. First, fire at the door and then eliminate the Stingers and company with some Homing Missiles and Super Laser firework. These guys have good aim, so you'll need to do some nifty dancing. After clearing the area, enter the area and hit the blue, glowing column. Now go back via way you came—to the amber-colored room. When you reach this room, you will notice three exits. Take the one that has a room with a blue, glowing structure.

Mission Seven

It's quite easy to get lost within the vast network of caverns below. To avoid this problem, always look for unique characteristics within each shaft and room. In addition, you can place markers along your path.

Head through the exit that has lights on each side (it's the only one with lights). The room you enter should have a speckled column (red, gray, green, blue, etc.). Proceed to the entrance up ahead until you spot a horizontally-elongated light to its left. Continue straight through these caverns until you reach a room containing a huge golden structure with blue side panels.

There are two entrances in this area, so take the right exit. This path leads to the Elevator Room, which is basically a shaft. Enter the open area in the structure, disposing of any lurking Bots. Then descend, but be warned that this is when things start to get crazy. There's a horde of Bots waiting, including some Gyros and Tubbs. Using your expertise and piloting skills, kill the menaces. Collect the **Concussion Missiles** and **Power-Ups**.

The chamber contains two switches, however, you need the Security Key. To get the key, take the right exit. This area curves to the left, and is patrolled by a Stinger and Gyro. Using the corner as a barrier, take out the two Bots. Continue along this path until you see a small chamber with an amber-colored glow. Take the **Microwave Cannon** to your right and destroy the Tubbs. Collect the **Energy Power-Ups** in the cubbyhole further to your right, and then continue through the shaft. The **Security Authorization Key** is easy to locate. It's that large, square-like object hovering in the middle of the air.

Collect the Key, but continue to move onward. Can you hear those eerie sounds, sort of a cyber siren? A Stinger is ahead. Take it out with your Homing Missiles, and then collect the **Power-Ups** along the way to the switches. Hit the switches to deactivate the force fields in the Virus Containment Room.

Head to the right, and continue until you see the small, amber-colored chamber. Now turn to the right and descend into the tiny cubbyhole. As you turn right again, you should notice that the force fields to the room are gone. Take note of the Stinger guarding the area, and eliminate it from outside the chamber.

Now that the area is clear, head inside. Now it's time to deactivate the Virus Containment Device. This is accomplished by looking near the small area with the flame jets. Then collect the two virus samples in the small area (where the flame jets were). These greenish-gray virus samples are octagon-shaped contraptions with rotating parts.

Hitting the switch (it has yellow and black markings) directly across from this area opens the ceiling hatch. Exit via this opening, and fly through the long shaft. This leads to a room with a rather hateful Squid, so send a Homing Missile its way. To your right is another shaft. This leads out, so take this path and blast off to victory, knowing that you've completed yet another grueling mission.

Mission Seven

Mission Eight

Although the new virus sample you provided gave us great data, it's going to take time to alter the anti-virus to make it effective. Destroying the fuel refinery at Dol Ammad on Europa should prove an excellent delaying tactic.

Also, there is a medical frigate holding some important scientists trapped at the facility. We need to get the scientists out so they can get to work on the antivirus. Your task is to rescue the scientists trapped in the medical frigate. When you free their ship, follow it out to safety.

Objectives

- Turn on cooling system
- Destroy the three heat sinks
- Find the medical frigate
- Release the medical frigate
- Escape

Enemies

- Thresher

Walkthrough

You're dropped off outside the refinery, which is well guarded.

Make your way to the three steam vents and enter any one of them. You'll probably need to use the Afterburner to make it past the steam flow. Upon entering the room at the bottom of the vent, you'll see a "welcoming committee" waiting to greet you with a myriad of weapons. Try sending a couple of Homing Missiles into the room to soften them up.

Go through the door near the floor of the steam room, and then drop to the floor of the room you just entered. There's another door behind you. Go through it to reach an intersection. Turn to the right and head down this corridor.

After a short distance down this corridor, you'll see a rotating cylinder with glowing red panels on it. In addition, it has a fire jet firing toward its single opening. Destroy all of the red panels to deactivate the fire jet, and then enter the cylinder.

There's a door at the bottom of the cylinder. Go through it and follow the snow tunnel. At the end of the tunnel you'll see another door with a small room beyond. Enter the room and flip the switch.

With the cooling system activated, one of the three main cooling towers is now open to evacuate waste heat from the refinery. Exit through the steam vents that you came in through.

After exiting the steam vents, position your craft so that the back of it faces the large communications antenna. When positioned correctly, head into the canyon to your right. The cooling tower, which you opened by activating the cooling system, is located at the end of the canyon. Take out as many of the Bots inside the tower as you can before entering so you can catch them off guard.

There's a glowing, rotating fan at the bottom of the cooling tower; however, it's protected by a force field. Flip the switch inside the tower, and then destroy the fan. (You can actually do this without entering the tower.) Destroying this cooling tower fan automatically kicks in the first backup tower.

Note

Just above the cooling fan's previous position, you can see four smaller fans set into the wall. There's a *Secret Area* behind each fan, each full of Power-Ups. Destroy the fans to get the goodies.

Leave the cooling tower and head back up the canyon. Stay to the left and enter another canyon. Follow this canyon to the first backup cooling tower, and employ the same routine on this tower that you used for the previous one. Note that this cooling tower has a gun emplacement outside, plus there are more robots inside.

Note

Because of their slow aiming speed, you can destroy gun emplacements more easily at close range. You can circle the gun by sliding from side to side while keeping your sites on the gun as you fire.

Tip

Don't forget about the *Secret Areas* behind the smaller fans in this cooling tower.

Once again, a backup tower is activated upon this tower's destruction. Take out the third cooling tower fan (and collect the **Power-Ups** in the *Secret Areas*) by exiting the tower, heading back up the canyon, and entering the canyon immediately to your left.

This tower has two gun emplacements located on either side of it. Take out these guns first, and then deal with the robots and glowing fan inside.

Now is your chance to become a hero. It's time to rescue the scientists being held hostage in the medical frigate.

There's a door leading into the facility near the secret area fans. Enter the door and head down the snow tunnel beyond.

Note

A short way down the tunnel, you'll reach an intersection with a cycling alert beacon. Take a left at the intersection and enter the room at its end. Destroy the Bots and flip the switch. Doing so causes the force field, that was once blocking the right-hand turn from the intersection, to drop. Return to the intersection and head up the other direction to enter a *Secret Area* with some Power-Ups.

Continue down the main tunnel until you spot a robot generator. Kill all the robots it creates; the generator will eventually run out of steam, enabling you to pass.

Go *very slowly* past the dead robot generator, because just past it there's a cooling fan room with an extremely powerful fan that will overpower your engines and suck you down into its blades. Reverse the fan's direction by flipping the switch across the room.

If you enter the room, you'll get blown toward the cooling system controller, along with a bunch of robots. Take out these robots, and the resulting explosions will help destroy the controller. This, in turn, will go tumbling down into the fan and destroy it.

Alternatively (and with much less risk), you can fire a few missiles into the room. They'll get blown toward the controller, eventually destroying it.

Mission Eight

Head down past where the big fan used to be, and enter the snow tunnel beyond. Continue down this tunnel until you reach a large room with a vertical cooling cylinder in it.

There's an ice cavern at the bottom of the room. Follow the cavern to its end; you should see a control tower with windows at the top—and a couple of gun emplacements. There's not much room to maneuver, so be careful when you take out the guns.

When the guns are gone, blast away one of the windows in the control tower. A couple of robots will come after you, so be prepared to destroy them immediately. Get them as they're exiting the window to limit their field of fire.

Enter the control tower, and head down the shaft at the back of the room. Go through the door at the bottom of the shaft, and then head up through the shaft you just entered. There's a room at the top of this shaft with damaged pipes spewing hot plasma.

After going through the door, you will enter another shaft. Head up this one, and continue up through more shafts until you reach the top. However, there's a robot generator waiting at the top. Get the generator in view, and then retreat down the shaft to limit the Bots' field of fire. Once the generator shuts down, go past it and through a few rooms until you reach a left-hand intersection.

To your left is the hangar where the medical frigate is docked. But beware—it's heavily guarded! Stay in the outer room while taking out individual robots as they appear.

You can't get the medical frigate out until you obtain the **Access Key**. Exit the hangar and turn to the left. Follow this corridor until it ends. Take a left and go through the door into another shaft. Go down the shaft and through the door at the bottom.

Now drop to the bottom of this room, and head down the new shaft. At the bottom of the shaft, go down the corridor through a few rooms until you reach a room with large glass windows set in the right-hand side. Behind the windows is a large cooling tube.

When you reach the hangar bay, enter the small control room just before the bay itself. Flip the large switch just inside the control room to release the elevator.

Follow the frigate up the elevator shaft, and protect it from the remaining Bots in the hangar. Also, keep an eye out for the gun emplacements at the top of the elevator shaft.

As you reach the top of the shaft, the frigate will begin its journey home. Follow them out to complete your mission.

Mission Eight

Mission Nine

Of course, you'd like a ship that's far more powerful than your current Pyro to help you battle the robot menace. Since we don't have the components to create a better ship, code-named Magnum, we'll steal them from P.T.M.C.

Your mission is to escort the covert cargo ship going in to recover the parts. Although direct assistance is helpful, creating a diversion is much more effective. (Plus, we can disrupt P.T.M.C.'s construction of more ships.)

Remember that cargo captains are not battle-hardened fighters like yourself and tend to overreact. When you receive a message saying that they're "in danger," you can pretty much ignore it. However, when they say that they're getting pummeled by P.T.M.C. forces, you need to help them as quickly as possible. Although using the covert transmitter (press "\") can help you find them, the Guide Bot is much quicker.

(This mission briefing assumes that the cargo ship is OK on its own. Since you will probably have to interrupt your quest to disrupt the stabilizers a couple of times, refer to your map often to determine the best path back to your next objective.)

Objectives

- Get the four seismic disrupters
- Disrupt the four seismic stabilizers
- Ensure that the covert cargo ship completes its mission

Enemies

- Spyhunter

Walkthrough

We'll drop you off outside the Mercury shipyards. Watch the cargo ship as it starts its way toward the entrance in direct sunlight. The flashes that you see are its ablative shielding being burned away. Take care to stay out of the sunlight as much as possible.

Move forward and drop off the right-hand side of bridge. Stay in the shadow and make your way to the second shipyard entrance. When your craft begins to smoke, adjust your position to stay in the shadow. Remember that the sun is coming from your left, so you want to stay somewhat to the right of the bridge.

Note

There are Power-Ups underneath the two entrances. In addition, there are some near the right-hand structure; however, the distance you need to travel to reach them will cause serious damage to your ship.

When you reach the entrance, quickly rise over the bridge and get inside quickly while taking care of the gun turrets mounted inside. (You might want to use your Afterburner for this.) Now make your way down the shaft to the bottom. When you reach the bottom, turn back in the direction where you left off and enter the rectangular shaft.

Follow the shaft to the bottom, and enter the room. When the door at the far end opens (due to the random firing between you and the robots), you'll get to see the first Seismic Stabilizer, or the Control Center Seismic Stabilizer. Ignore it for now while you take out the robots in this room.

Mission Nine

Once the robots are gone, drop to the bottom of the room to find the four **Seismic Disrupters**. Grab all four of them and head into the Control Center Seismic Stabilizer room.

Flip the switch on the wall beyond the stabilizer, and then get close to the stabilizer. Select one of the disrupters from your inventory and release it. This causes the stabilizer to malfunction and alarm claxons will wail. Only three more stabilizers to go. The first one to go after is the storage stabilizer.

Exit the room and go through the second door on the right. Go up the shaft and exit into the large storage room. Watch out for the robots and the four gun turrets across the room. There are small passageways on either side of the gun turrets. Go through either one of these passageways into the next large storage room. Again, watch out for more robots and go through the passageways at the far end of the room into *another* storage room.

This storage room has two doors where the passageways were in the first two. Go through the right-hand door into the Storage Stabilizer room. Flip the switch and drop another Seismic Disrupter near the stabilizer. Ah, the joyous sounds of claxons as you watch the stabilizer arcing because of the disruptions. Two down, two to go!

Next on the list is the Factory Seismic Stabilizer. Exit the stabilizer room, and head straight across the storage room through the passageway. Go to the last storage room and drop about halfway down. Head into the passageway, but beware of the robots and the gun turrets at the end of the passageway.

At the end of the passageway, exit to the right and rise up toward the intersection ahead of you. Again, watch out for gun turrets and robots in the room beyond the intersection.

Go through the intersection into the factory room beyond the intersection. Drop into the shaft to the left of the intersection. The third stabilizer should now be in front of you.

Once again, flip the switch and drop off a disrupter. Only one more to go!

Exit the stabilizer room and return to the factory floor. Exit to your left, and head back to the intersection. Follow the curving corridor until you reach a large shaft.

Enter the shaft, which is also curved, and follow it to the bottom. This large, intersecting chamber is well defended, so watch it! There are many gun turrets and robots to contend with.

After clearing out this room, head to the right-hand, downward curving shaft. About halfway down, you'll see the Assembly Stabilizer, which is the fourth and final stabilizer. Note that there are four of these shafts, each of which has a room halfway down.

Note

If you get disoriented during the firefight with the robots, keep trying each of the shafts until you find the right one.

Mission Nine

Now you can concentrate your energy on protecting the cargo ship. Have the guide Bot direct you to it.

Note While escorting the ship, it's a good idea to turn on your "review mirror" to keep your eye on the ship more easily. Press *Shift* + *F1* or *Shift* + *F2* to place the reverse view in either your left- or right-hand display panel respectively.

Other than taking out every robot that gets in the way of the cargo ship, the only tricky part of protecting the ship occurs when it reaches a series of force fields.

The first danger occurs courtesy of the large "horse" robot. This thing is huge and bursting with weapons. Luckily, it's also extremely slow, so if you keep moving you can avoid its guns. If you have some Mega Missiles, these will also do the trick. Without them, you must continually pummel it with whatever you have in your arsenal.

Unfortunately, the cargo ship is too big to get through the small passageways at the top of the room on either side of the force field. It must wait on you to disable the force field. Go through either passageway into the room beyond. Take out the lurking Bots before disabling the force field.

To disable the force field, flip the switches on each side of the force field. As the force field drops, the cargo ship will enter the new room. However, there's another force field at the far end of the room.

Enter the far room using the corresponding passageways, but *don't deactivate the force field* right away. Directly ahead of the force field is a small alcove containing the next component that the cargo ship will pick up. Unfortunately, this alcove is heavily guarded. Take out the Bots and gun turrets in the alcove and the main room before opening the second force field.

Note

There are a bunch of Power-Ups below the next component. If you're a little low on supplies, pick them up while the cargo ship picks up its component.

The cargo ship will now head for the next component, and then return to the surface with it. Escort it to the drop-off point, and then make sure that it doesn't get obliterated while it picks up the last piece of equipment. Follow it out to the surface to complete this mission.

Mission Nine

Mission Ten

We'll sneak you into a low security hangar in the C.E.D. Lunar Command Center on the moon. From there, you'll need to find a way to upload our data into their mainframe. We'll jam surface transmissions as much as possible to keep the station from going on alert.

If we can do this, the C.E.D. will be convinced that Dravis and P.T.M.C. need to be dealt with. We will also no longer be viewed as terrorists.

Good Luck.

Objectives

- Infiltrate the Lunar Command Center
- Obtain Data Vault Key
- Enter Data Vault
- Acquire Data Interface
- Initialize Data Interface
- Connect to Data Uplink

Enemies

- Pest
- Thiefbot
- Tailbot
- Hood
- Stinger
- Orbot
- Gyro
- Omegatrooper
- Stormtrooper
- Flak
- Tracker
- Banshee
- Juggernaut
- Squid

Walkthrough

Turn your ship 180 degrees to face the mother ship behind you. See the pillar to the left of the ship? There is a hovering Security Camera Monitor in front of it. Grab it. Below that is the **hangar message log**. Download the data from that site by pressing Shift and F8.

Note

Records will inform you that a security camera malfunctioned in the hangar area, resulting in the damaging of a ship. The craft's remains have been shipped to an old mine.

Shoot out the cameras and turrets situated in each corner of the room. Weave in and out from under the canopy, taking each out with your Laser. There are two doors in the hangar, but only one is unlocked. The elongated purple door is impassable. Thus, you must pass through the yellow and black hatch. Head down the chute, which dumps you into a blue tunnel. Head to your right, hugging the wall to avoid an army of Pests that lie ahead.

Tip

This place is heavily infested with Pests. Take out as many as you can by nestling the wall and sniping each. Trying to fight all of them at the same time is impossible.

Kill the Pests, then mop up the Thiefbot, (i.e., the green crab-like critter). It is quite a flyer, so you're in for a chase. Also, it takes several shots with the Laser to destroy. But once it's gone, you're rewarded with some nice stolen **items**.

Enter the angular entrance ahead, careful just to peep through. Take out a few Tailbots with your Laser. Keep an eye out to your left. The Tailbots like to ambush you from that point. When you're spotted, rush out into the tunnel (where you killed the Pests). Shoot the Tailbots while backing up from the critters, luring as many out as possible. Once you have mopped them up, head inside.

Mission Ten

Obtain the **Ship Message Log** containing recon pilot T. Murphy's SOS. Collect the **Mass Driver** and **Power-Ups**. Creep into the dark blue crevice to your right. Grab the **Homing Missile** and ascend the shaft above. The next area is an old, abandoned chamber. No action in here; it's time to head outside. Put on the Cloak and slip out the hole in the ceiling.

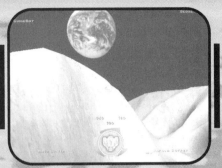

Note

As you exit, mountains stretch behind you, while part of the base lies ahead. Find a niche in one of the valleys in the mountain range (near a protruding pipe). There are all kinds of goodies in here, from Cyclone Missiles to Chaff Packs. Collect them and head back out, saving the Cloak for last.

Slip on a Cloak and step into the Afterburner. Streak across the plain (where part of the base resides), into the valley across from where you first popped up. Pass the picturesque rotunda, continuing through the valley. After several zigzags, you'll meet two groups of Tanks (two in each group). Take them out with your Vauss.

You can navigate the final mountain on this leg of the journey from either side. Although the right path is easier than the left, neither will be a cakewalk.

Note

Going left takes you to a campground and the Juggernaut. Unfortunately, this Goliath of machines is impossible to take down. And when it gets to camp, giant Jugger will notify the base of your intrusion.

Move right, slowing up as you catch sight of a large structure. The building is armed to the teeth. In fact, a big gun that will take a hefty load of points off your shields is attached nearby. Be careful! Watch out for a platoon of Bots and Tanks guarding this area. Use your missiles on these guys, dodging in and out of the mountains and valleys.

Once the area is clear, put on the Afterburner and make a run for it, heading for the far right of the building. Tanks dot the mountainside; send missiles their way. Once across, nestle below, near the base of the structure. No guns can reach you here. Take out the rest of the Tanks.

Head slightly past the structure, wary of the guns. Be sure to use the Afterburner. The Data Link Building is directly "north" of this compound.

Tip

The compound's guns are powerful and accurate. Better to take on the Tanks, which are larger, slower moving targets. So move out from the structure in a two o'clock manner, skimming the mountain to your right.

Smoke the Banshee, and then cruise into the valley ahead. The Data Link building is located here. First, though, you must mop up the guarding Bots. Once you do that, grab the **Data Vault Key**. It's inside the column connected to the building. The column's entry point is near its base on the opposite side. Watch out for the guns. Take out the lower two with the Vauss. Next, open the hatch. Ascend to the Key. After that, descend and enter the large portal outside the column door. This is the Data Vault.

Take out the Manta Ray. Descend to the large, circular room below. Prepare for battle. Take out the Omega Troopers, Squids, and Stingers. Head toward the door, the one without red lights. The red-lit portal is full of Bots and matcens; more Squids will enter your current area from there, so beware.

Enter. Take out the Manta Rays, heading left. This room is large and has numerous portals. Take the door to your immediate left. There is a **Data Link** on the far side of the room. Download the information. You'll find out that this is the Data Interface Prep Room. Prep your ship by entering the initializing Hub in the center of this room. Once completed, leave the room.

Mission Ten

If the Orbots are driving you mad. Hit the switches behind the matcen. This will stop their production.

Head into the large, circular room with numerous portals. Descend into the long, yellow, glowing shaft. Take out the enemy Bots in the elongated room from which this shaft leads. Toward the other end lies an extended "arm" with a weird-looking **Power-Up** at the end of it. Above the "arm" is a **Data Link**. Access it.

Note

Certain Data Interfaces may require a Memory Plasma Charge in order to connect successfully to the Main Uplink Center. This arm-like device will continually generate charges for this purpose.

Wait to mess with the Memory Plasma Generator. Head to the nearby door. Do not enter. Two Storm Troopers lurk directly under the entrance. Take them out from the portal, and then enter. This is a large room. Ascend above to collect the **hidden goodies**. Axe the Sharcs and Manta Rays.

Descend back down to where you destroyed the Storm Troopers. There is a doorway straight ahead. Enter. Gather the **Energy Power-Ups** within the pink-lit area. Just ahead, though, are two powerful turret guns guarding the blue area. Take them out from afar using your Guided Missiles. Progress to the blue area; gather up the **Homing Missiles** down below.

Proceed through the next entrance. Beware of the descending red mines. Using your Omega Cannon, clear a path out to the **Data Link**. Download the information and quickly run back to the other room to read the message so as not to be hit by a mine.

Note

The room with all those mines is the Data Uplink Center. Once Uplink Control has authorized your upload, you may dock with the Data Uplink by positioning your ship directly between the plasma nodes.

Head back to the Data Uplink Center, plowing your way through the mines. Ascend to the top area of the room. Behind you are glass panels. Send a missile through one. Be careful entering. Two turrets are stationed to your immediate left and right. Take these suckers out.

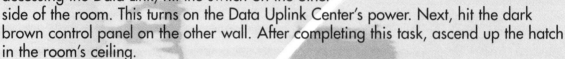

To your right is another **Data Link**. Access it. The Link lists some directives. Once you've finished accessing the Data Link, hit the switch on the other side of the room. This turns on the Data Uplink Center's power. Next, hit the dark brown control panel on the other wall. After completing this task, ascend up the hatch in the room's ceiling.

A huge welcoming party is there to greet you, consisting primarily of Squids. Send some Napalm and Homing Missiles their way. Collect the **goodies** in the room, and then head out the door nearest to the hole from which you entered.

Just what you needed—another welcoming party! Blast away at the Squids and Stingers. Toward the back of the matcen are two switches. Hit them to deactivate Bot production. Enter the adjoining room. To your left are three pillars with monitors. On the back of each is a switch. Hit all three.

Note

You have 30 seconds to make it from the Memory Plasma Generator Room to the two crystal blue plasma nodes before the Plasma Power-Up Pass expires.

Head back to the Memory Plasma Generator room. Grab the funny-looking **Power-Up**. Rush to the Data Link room, kicking in the Afterburner. Fly as fast as you can to the nodes. They are two large, blue panels sandwiching volts of blue electricity. When you reach the nodes, the level is complete.

Mission Ten

Mission Eleven

Dravis has captured one of our pilots. Because of the sensitive information that the pilot knows, it's imperative that you release him and his ship from the P.T.M.C. Storage Facility on Titan.

Objectives

- Open blocked tunnel
- Destroy force field generators
- Release the prisoner
- Guard his getaway

Enemies

- Surveillance Turret
- GTZ-34 Gun Turret
- MT-A1 Gun Turret

Walkthrough

We'll drop you off outside the facility. Directly in front of you, you'll see a main tower protected by gun turrets on three of its six sides. Make your way past the tower to the small entrance bunker beyond. The entry doorways immediately behind the tower are locked, and we haven't obtained the Access Keys for you.

Enter the bunker and head straight down the tunnel until you reach a large room with mining cart tracks. There is a cart on one of the tracks. If you feel like creating some mayhem, flip the switch beneath the cart to send it careening down the tracks, where it will hit a pile of rocks and explode. You can get past this cave in without letting loose the cart, however.

Note
If you're running low on supplies, visit the cave to pick up some much needed Power-Ups.

Go down the tunnel that the cart was in, and head into the hole in the floor. At the bottom of the hole is another set of tracks. One path is blocked, while the other path has another cart. Release the cart and let it smash into the group of rocks blocking the other end of the tunnel.

Note
Don't get in the way of the cart while it's on its way. The explosion caused by the cave-in can cause damage to your ship.

Head into the newly opened tunnel, and proceed down the shaft at its end. While in the shaft, you should spot an opening. The Bots in this room are hiding in two alcoves. By using stealth, however, you can dispose of at least one from the relative safety of the shaft before entering the room.

Mission Eleven

There are two shafts set into either side of the room. Take either one down to the room below, and then go through the door into the curving passageway. Quickly get to the ceiling directly between the two gun turrets (you'll need to use your Afterburner in this situation). This places your ship out of their field of fire, plus you can easily destroy them both.

Note

There is some data on your computer showing the surveillance cameras so you can recognize them. This data is automatically displayed when you enter the curving passageway.

Continue down the passageway until you reach the two force field generators. These two generators appear to be decoys, so you can destroy them at your discretion. If you elect not to destroy them, they'll serve as a good landmark when you return later.

There's a small orange room opposite the generators. Enter the room and open the door in the ceiling. Doing so reveals a very tall shaft. Immediately inside the door are two Bots. The big problem, however, are the two gun turrets at the top of the shaft, which is where you need to go. Launch a couple of Homing Missiles from the safety of the doorway, and move into position to fire. Once that's done, use your craft's Afterburner to reach the top of the shaft before the gun turrets can hit you.

There's a small alcove at the top with a force field at one end. Take out the Bots, and then flip the switch. You should be able to take out the gun turrets without a problem.

Head back down the shaft and return to the curving corridor. Turn to the left and head back the way you came. Take the first left in the corridor, and head into the circular room with three exits (you came in through one of them). Go through the right-hand exit.

Take out the three gun turrets. You can get the closest one (in the ceiling on the way into the room) quickly before it even knows you're there. This will set off the second one directly behind it. Nail the second one quickly with some fast laser fire or Homing Missiles (if you have them). The third turret is located at the right-hand end of the room. If you stay behind the supports, and slide out to take pot shots at it, you can destroy it. Watch out for the Bot in the room while you're doing this.

There's a switch across the room from the third turret. After flipping the switch, head back out to the circular room and into the right-hand exit (it was the left-hand exit when you first entered the room). Hang a right into the corridor that you encounter. Now blow up the generator you come to, and drop the force field directly behind it.

Go through where the force field was previously located, and destroy the Bots—but *don't take out the cameras*. Flip the three switches that are located next to each other. This will make the primary force field generators vulnerable.

Note

After disposing of the Bots, go to the force fields that are approximately one-quarter and halfway around the room from where you came in. For each force field, do the following:

Flip the switch over the camera and toss a few flares at the force field. Watch the fun as the five gun turrets across the room fire at the force field generator and blow it up. Make sure you get out of the way when the force field drops!

After destroying the generator, the turrets will continue to fire and destroy their surveillance camera. Dismantle any remaining Bots, and then head into the room with the turrets. Quickly get onto the shelf above the guns and take out the remaining Bots. Now go to the ceiling and move backwards toward the entrance with your ship pointing down toward the guns. When you can see the guns, destroy each one in turn. Go around the room and pick up the Power-Ups.

Exit the room and then head back out of the ring-shaped room the same way you entered. Now return to the circular room with three exits, and destroy the three (previously invulnerable) force field generators. This will deactivate the force field at the top of this room.

Go up through where the force field was. While keeping a watchful eye on any Bots, go up one of the vertical shafts located along the sides of the room. When you reach the next level (this one resembles a doughnut), you'll notice a locked door—remember its location!

Go through one of the corridors that leads into the center of the doughnut-like room, and then head upward.

Note

About halfway up the shaft, you'll spot a switch. Behind the switch, there's a *Secret Area* with some worthwhile Power-Ups.

Leave the *Secret Area* and quickly get above the gun turrets at the top of this area. After eliminating the gun turrets and annoying Bots, grab the **Hub Security Key** resting in this area.

Head up to the room directly above you, and quickly get to the ledge above the guns at the end of the room. Turn around and flip the switch directly in front of you, and then take out the guns from the safety of the ledge.

Note

There's a force field generator above the guns. Destroy it to open the force fields below. These force fields protect the *Secret Areas*.

Repeat the above process at the other end of the room. You'll need to use your craft's Afterburners to get through relatively unscathed.

Head back down the shaft in the center of the room, and go down about halfway. This should take you to the switch that you flipped earlier. Go through the door opposite the switch. (Flipping the switched unlocked it.)

After eliminating the Bots, flip the two switches directly above the door you came in. Now exit the door opposite where you came in. This will take you to yet another doughnut-shaped corridor.

Continue around until you reach a door in the ceiling. After entering a circular shaft, go all the way up the shaft as far as possible. This takes you to a room with four exits near the ceiling. These four exits access yet another doughnut-shaped corridor; however, this one is heavily defended with gun turrets and robots. Take them out, but be very careful about it.

Note

When you look through an exit for the first time, you'll see more automated data indicating that the force field generators you see must be destroyed.

First, from the safety of the central room, destroy the four surveillance cameras visible from the exits. Doing so will slow down the turrets' reaction time. Now, using quick out-and-in motions, head into the corridor, blast a gun, and return to the central room before you get hit. Repeat this a number of times until both guns are history.

Now you can use the relatively fire-free zone as a base to work your way around this area. Quickly flip the switches in the corridor. You must be quick because the switches will reset if you fail to activate them quickly enough. The best way to do this is to slide around the corridor while continually aiming toward the center. When a switch comes into view, hit it with a flare.

When you've flipped all six switches, the force field generators will be vulnerable. Destroy them.

Behind one of the generators, you'll find the ship you've been looking for. Flip the switch in the ceiling above it to free the ship. Follow it out and protect it from any remaining Bots.

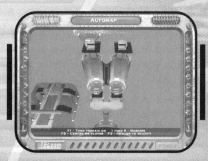

For security reasons, only one of the doors will open when one ship is in front of it. Turn around when the pilot tells you to and head out through the exit opposite it.

Sorry, but there's no way to prevent what happens next...

Mission Eleven

Mission Twelve

Objectives

- Escape from the fire trap
- Acquire Level Keys 1 through 4
- Eliminate Championship Competitors
- Defeat the Proving Grounds Champion
- Escape from the Proving Grounds

Enemies

- Gyro
- Orbot
- Tailbot
- Sparky
- Gunslinger
- Stinger
- Squid
- Thresher
- Dragon

Walkthrough

Talk about being stuck between a rock and a hard place. Beginning this mission harnessed in a Torture Mechanism while being hung over a lava pit describes this situation well. Although you can't move, you must act quickly. Before you become burnt toast, take out the five flame jet throwers.

Note

The middle flamethrower is the largest and most damaging of the Torture Mechanism's sadistic weaponry. Unfortunately, you usually have to knock out the other four before taking out the Big Daddy.

After extinguishing the fires, begin to unleash yourself from the beam generators. You can do this by firing into the force fields (speckled pink panels on both sides of the Torture Mechanism), which causes the firepower to ricochet off and disable the beam generator.

Tip

Fire upon the mid-section of the very far right of the right force field. After several shots, the beam will disappear. Next, fire upon the mid-section of the very far left of the left force field, disabling the other beam.

You're free! Gather the **Power-Ups**, **Cloak**, and **Frag Missiles** in each of the rooms. Also, make sure you look in the shafts. It doesn't matter which shaft you take, because both lead to the same chamber.

Take the large exit in the next chamber, continuing straight through several rooms until you reach a dead end. Be careful in the first room, because

Mission Twelve

there are a horde of Bots, from Stingers to Gyros. They will appear from both side entrances. Remember the Roman coliseum and the lions? If so, you get the picture!

Tip

If you pick up the **Cloak** Power-Up last from all the goodies in the torture chamber, you can rush past this point without getting attacked. Using your Afterburner is not a bad idea either.

Once you reach the dead end, look up, and ascend to the small chamber. Watch out for the lurking Tubbs. To your back-left is a P.T.M.C. door, so enter it. Take out the Gyro, and collect the goodies. Then disable the security force field by pressing the switch.

Return to the room with the shaft in the floor, but prepare for the fight of your life. Bots will attack from just about every direction, so make a mad dash for the shaft. However, don't think that you can escape the enemy barrage of firepower that easily. More Bots lurk below, so zoom through the door.

Hang a right, and dispose of any Bots that you see in the distance. Keep going until you reach a portal on your right and a switch to your left. Flip the switch to unlock the door, and then enter. Take the goodies in the blue areas, but make sure you destroy the turrets first. Now leave this area.

Note

This path contains areas that fork. Fortunately, these paths are circular in nature and meet one another. Don't worry; you can't get lost!

Proceed down the path. As it curves left, take out the Orbot and the two Tailbots. Stop at the next switch and door location if you think you need more weapon Power-Ups. Hit the switch and enter. A **Fusion Cannon** and **Plasma Cannon** await below. Take out the two turrets and gather the goodies.

Continue until you reach another fork in the path (remember, the paths are connected). Find the next switch and portal combination. If you take a left, they are to your right. You can't miss them—the area is surrounded by Gunslingers and Tailbots. Shoot them down, press the switch, and then enter.

You're now in the *Level 1 Arena* in a death match with one bad Stinger. He won't go down as easily as the others. Jab him with a couple of Laser shots, and then deliver the knockout punch—a Frag Missile. Of course, you'll need to bob and weave like the Heavyweight Champion if you're gonna survive.

Mission Twelve

After taking out Stinger, ascend through the hatch in the ceiling. Hang a right, wary of the Gunslingers to the left, and then take another right. The **Level 2 Key** is at the end of this tunnel. Grab it and head back.

A group of Squids are waiting near the intersection, so gun them down. The Level 2 area is in this tunnel. You will pass an Energy Center on your right, so go there and recharge. Continue down the winding corridor, taking the next right. This is the where the Level 2 chamber begins.

Gather the goodies, and then descend to the floor. Take the exit under the platform, wary of the lurking Bots. Axe the Gunslingers and Stinger, and then collect the goodies. Check in every nook and cranny, because these things are hidden well.

Tip

This room has some rowdy characters. Rather than entering the hornets' nest, take on each one from the portal. This will prevent them from ganging up on you.

Enter the door ahead, but prepare yourself for the Level 2 Thresher Boss. Ascend to the top level to greet him. Don't waste your Laser or EMP Gun on this guy; it will take missiles to get the job done. Frags and Smart Missiles are fine, but the Mega Missile is, by far, your best bet.

Remember that classic scene in *Raiders of the Lost Ark* when Indiana Jones pulls out his pistol and takes down the ominous sword-swinging assassin? Well, send a Mega Missile the Boss' way, and watch him disappear faster than Indiana's foe.

There's a ceiling hatch over the acid pit. Go ahead and enter it, and dispose of the pesky turret gun, Manta Rays, and Tailbots. Gather the goodies under what remains of the turret gun, and head to the left. Take out the horde of Bots guarding the door. An Energy Center is on the other side. After recharging your shields, hit the switch.

Ready for a showdown? There's a Gunslinger waiting in Arena 3. Fire some missiles into the Bot to show it who's the boss. It will usually take a few missiles to eliminate this Gunslinger. However, note that energy-based weapons take even longer.

Taking the next door will bring you to the Proving Grounds for Arena 4, which is crowded with numerous Bots. Press the switch on the wall near the yellow, cylinder-shaped reactor. Collect the key, and then shoot out the three orange boxes surrounding the cylinder. This will deactivate the force fields.

Head to the right, and dismantle the Bots guarding the doorway. After entering the doorway, prepare to battle a killer Tailbot. It's mean and tempestuous, and won't wait for you to deliver the first "punch." However, one hit with your Impact Mortar will put it in its place.

Mission Twelve

Next, enter the corridor from which you came, avoiding the temptation to descend to the floor hatch. Head to the left arena. Take out the Stinger and Gunslinger, and then prepare for a second Level 4 death match. Handle this guy the same way as you did the first.

Note

After destroying the second Tailbot Boss, you are granted access to all areas.

Enter the newly opened corridor. This area looks like a mirror version of the one with the orange reactor. Smoke the two Gunslingers and the Thresher, head to the left, and then collect the old Data Cartridge at the end of the area. Return to either of the Tailbot Boss rooms and go down the floor shaft.

The championship arena has four competitors waiting within the inner ring. Eliminate them all to deactivate the force field blocking your entry onto the next level. Collect the goodies (including a **Mega Missile**) along the outer corridor, and then prepare for the supreme death match.

Tip

If you dispose of one or two of the competitors, sometimes the others fight amongst themselves. If so, just let them annihilate each other.

Descend through the floor shaft to meet the ultimate terror—Dragon. This spider-like machine is practically invincible, however, it does have one weakness. Its abdomen's orifice is vulnerable to Impact Mortars. Try to sneak in a mortar, although you must be wary of the four blades guarding it.

Tip

Fly over this monstrosity and launch an Impact Mortar within the triangular orifice on the back of its abdomen. This will set off plenty of fireworks.

Note

They don't call this Boss the Dragon for nothing. If you get too close, it will propel a huge torch of Napalm your way.

After destroying this killing machine's abdomen, fire a couple of missiles to rid yourself of its crawling torso. Victory is yours! You're the king of the world! Escape through a ceiling chute and celebrate.

Mission Twelve

Mission Thirteen

The CED has publicly announced that a meeting with the so-called "terrorists" will be held aboard the Flagship Carrier Expediator. This is an obvious signal to us that they want to discuss the data and its implications. Fly to the Expediator and meet with the CED Officers to discuss the Dravis Conspiracy.

Objectives

- Destroy Stormtrooper leader
- Disable aft matcen
- Shut down engine core

Enemies

- Flametrooper
- Supertrooper
- Orbot
- Gyro
- Squid
- Old Scratch
- Manta Ray

Walkthrough

To your left is a **Smart Missile**. After you pick it up, turn around and take in the area behind you. To your right is a multi-layered platform. Collect the **Napalm Fuel** on each platform. There are some goodies hidden behind this platform, including some **Power-Ups**, **Concussion Missiles**, and **Cyclone Missiles**.

Fly through the rest of the hangar section (the area with the celestial ceiling view). There are some more "Easter Eggs" in this chamber, including a **GunBoy** and many **Missiles**. Grab these goodies and prepare to set off.

Tip

Look all around for goodies—near the ceiling, in lower realms, and in every nook and cranny. Load up on free stuff!

Shoot at the exit at the opposite end of the multi-layered platform. After blasting a couple of Squids, clean up the **Power-Ups**. Enter the next door through a hallway that curves to the left. Continue along this path until you reach an intersection. Beware of the two Squids lurking to the right, and dispose of them with your Laser.

Continue straight, grab the **Impact Mortar**, and then take the door. Christmas has come early! Gather all of the goodies you can. There is even a Shield Recharging Center. If you enter within the purple panels, you can charge your Shields up to 200 points. Don't enjoy yourself too much here, though; you have a job to do.

Return to the intersection, and head down the right passageway where the two Squids were. Enter the door, but beware of the Bots. Clean them up, and then continue down the shaft. Some Flametroopers and other Bots await; rain on their parade and collect their weapons.

Enter the next door, but watch out for a Supertrooper. Blast it as well as that pesky turret with your new Omega Gun. There's another door towards the upper-right wall. Take out the Sparky, and collect the **Guided Missile Pack**. Access the Data Link to your right to reveal where the aft matcen switch is located.

Tip
Occasionally, before you reach the Data Link building, one or two Scratches may sneak up on you.

Go back out. To your right is a green Banshee, so eliminate it. To your left is the door from which you entered; look above that portal to see a small shaft. It's so small, in fact, that your fighter will not be able to go in. This duct leads to the aft matcen switch. Aim a Guided Missile toward the pinkish-red area, and steer the missile to the right so that it hits the switch. If you need more Guided Missiles, they will continue to appear in the Data Link room.

Aiming the Guided Missile can be difficult. Using the full Guided Missile view makes things easier. You can do this by going to the "General" section under "Options."

After activating the switch, enter the hatch from which you first entered this chamber. Return to the intersection, and take the tunnel that descends below at the point of the intersection. There's also an Energy Center there, so recharge if necessary. Continue down the tunnel until you tumble down the hatch in the ceiling.

To your right is another Bot. Eliminate it for giggles, and pick up the Napalm Rocket. Shoot the metallic crates for Energy Power-Ups.

Do not go through the door on your right. Instead, turn left but don't go very far because two Supertroopers are waiting. Instead, descend below in the pink-lit shaft from the floor. Take out the two lurking Bots—they love to hide on the tunnel beams. When you reach the room, swing left down the tunnel.

Mission Thirteen

Enter the door with the octagon-shaped portal, but beware of several Bots lurking ahead (including Orbots, and a few Manta Rays). Clean up the area, and then continue on with your mission.

Note

To your left is a matcen panel that will continue to produce Orbots, regardless of how many you kill. Get used to it; this place is full of robot-producing matcens!

Hang a right. This tunnel is full of steam—and Orbots. Take the door and continue until you reach a junction. Descend through the shaft in the floor. This connects to a small, pink-lit area with a lurking Sparky. Smoke this baddie and move into the "high-heat" cubbyhole. Descend from that point slightly to the edge leading into the blue chamber. This is where the engines are located.

Note

There are three jet exhausts that fire every few seconds. The power of the thrust will push back your Pyro GL. You must get the timing correct, flying up the bottom one into the room. Also, keep in mind that the engines fire for about 8 seconds, and rest for 5.

This act will require the use of your Afterburner. When launching from the "red room," carefully avoid the protruding ventilation system. One bump and you can forget about making it. Slip into the propulsion area, and then rush up to avoid the exhaust engine's fire.

When you reach the inside of the reactor room, hit the three switches with your Laser to deactivate the reactor. Two doors lead out of the room, but both are locked. In the hallway, though, is a **Full Map Power-Up**.

Mission Thirteen

Mission Fourteen

The C.E.D.'s strategic orbital platform is offline. The entire defense net communications are maintained from this platform.

We'll start you off inside the station. We don't know the extent of the damage. You may need to re-align the mirror nodes and get the systems back online before you broadcast the anti-virus.

Objectives

- Find escape shuttle
- Find Equipment Room Key
- Find three bypass connectors
- Start Transmitter Control System
- Upload anti-virus program
- Enable Defense Network Output
- Deactivate Beam Emitter Shield
- Align mirror nodes
- Ignite beam emitter
- Ensure success of transmission
- Successfully broadcast anti-virus program

Enemies

- Sharc
- Stinger
- Squid
- Tailbot
- Supertrooper
- Flametrooper
- Watcher
- Barnswallow
- Thiefbot
- Hunter

Walkthrough

Another precarious beginning! Blow away the Sharc and collect the **Concussion Missiles**. Descend to the lower part of the chamber, and then shoot out the boxes and crates to pick up the **Anti-Virus Program** and some **Power-Ups**. Take the entrance.

Head down the first tunnel chamber; there are no Bots waiting. The next tunneled chamber contains three Sharcs. Show them who's boss, then keep on truckin'. A room with four entrances is ahead.

Note

Sharcs can't fire weapons, but they do have a serious bite. If they make contact with your ship, you'll lose 10 points from your shields.

A red Stinger, located on one of the ceiling beams, guards the room. Blast it to smithereens using two or three Concussion Missiles. After mopping up this menace, take the door straight ahead. Continue until you reach another room.

Tip

One tunneled section contains four Sharcs. Dodge in and out of the portal to destroy these critters. Never take on a group of these guys at one time.

There's a body on the floor, and above it is the Data Technician's Journal. After collecting and reading it, you uncover that a virus has infected one of the data links this scientist was trying to fix. Keep your eyes open. Many other clues will appear throughout this mission.

Ascend through the ceiling opening. This small room contains a Data Link, but it's broken. Axe the Sharc and Barnswallow, and then blow away the boxes inside the room for some **Power-Ups**. Head through the side tunnel adjoining this room. Blow up the boxes and other miscellaneous stuff blocking your way so you can pick up the Log and the **Afterburner Cooler**.

Mission Fourteen

Note

The Log is an extension of the one discovered earlier. According to the journal, this technician was stationed on Beam Ignition duty during his first day.

Return to the room with the Sharc matcen. Take out any "jaws" in your path, and then ascend through the ceiling exit. This area resembles a greenhouse that contains loads of Bots, including Squids and Sharcs. Cleanse the area of these critters, giving this lovely location a much-needed vacation from evil. Take out the Squids with your Homing Missiles first, saving the Lasers for the Sharcs.

Tip

The Bypass Connector is located near the body of water. This gadget will fix the broken Data Link.

Descend back into the room with the Sharc matcen. Touch the Data Link and you'll find that it now operates properly. Return to the room with the four entrances. Hang a left and collect the **Equipment Room Key**, as well as the **Power-Up** and **Vauss Rounds**.

Head back to the room from which you came, but this time continue straight. The next room contains a slain figure with a Beam Security Journal. The log states that: "The last time we tried to broadcast, an infected robot almost took out the emitter lens!" Some virus! In this same room, proceed through the floor hatch. The doorway connects to a large, empty warehouse-like area with another door. Exit. An even larger room awaits you.

This area is enormous. In fact, it is comprised of three levels. You begin on the middle level, with the goal of rising to the upper realm. There's a switch in this compartment near the top corner of this room. Hit it to release the shuttle. Descend down the force-fielded pipe, and then enter the pipe by ascending to the top of the room. Keep a watchful eye out for the Bot waiting in there.

Note

An Energy Center, as well as some menacing Sharcs, are on the third level.

The Data Connector is in the adjoining room. First, take out three Supertroopers followed by the Sharcs. Here's how: Nestle under the protruding arcs near the lobby floor. This will provide some protection while pounding the Supertroopers. With no more Supertroopers, move out to mop up the Sharcs.

Grab the **Data Collector**, and then head down the right hallway; however, *do not* enter the chamber. Take out as many Bots as possible from the opening. There's an assortment of machines guarding this area, including Tailbots, Supertroopers, Sharcs, and a Flametrooper.

After cleaning up this small army of troops, repair the Data Link inside this room. This is accomplished by simply touching the Data Link. After collecting the **Engineering Room Report,** you discover that the new transmitter output selection system, a clock-like dial in the lower engineering room, is ready to target networks.

Collect the **Beam Shield Deactivation Code** on the other side of room. (The code is NW - SE - W - NE.) After taking these two items (the Engineering Room Report and the Beam Shield Deactivation Code), return to the three-leveled area. Remember that the exit can only be accessed from the second level. Leave this area and make way for the room with four entrances.

Proceed through the ceiling hatch, wary of the Squid guarding the place. Destroy it and collect the **Power-Ups**. This room has three special shock pads consisting of **Shield Power-Ups**, **Smart Missiles**, and **Napalm Fuel**. You need to carefully "land" on top of each so as to avoid damage to your Shields (each "shock" causes about 3 points of damage).

Ascend through next hatch. After defeating the Squid and Watcher, ascend again to an open area in the top of this chamber. You may have to look around a bit, but it's there. This corridor has a fork in its path; take the left path. This will lead you to the log entry and the emitter lens.

Note

A matcen is located on the left hallway. Take out as many Bots as needed and zoom through the door ahead.

Mission Fourteen

As you scoop the lens, blast the Stingers that will appear. Two matcens are up ahead. One produces Mega Missiles, while the other spits out Squids. Collect as many **Mega Missiles** as possible. Also, try to avoid the Squid long enough so that you can collect the other goodies (such as **Homing Missiles**, **Afterburner Cooler**, and the next **Ship Message Log**).

Note

The Log reports an incident involving infected Bots. As a result, the station's power is turned off.

Return to the hallway junction from which you came, except this time head straight. Collect the **Vauss** and other goodies along the way. Don't forget to shoot up the boxes for **Power-Ups**. In fact, the third **Bypass Connector** is hidden behind these boxes. After collecting it, cut off the three matcen power switches.

Go back to the junction, but this time go to the right. Ascend into the large room, taking out the Stinger, Sharc, and Squid. Touch the Data Link to start the Transmitter Control System, and then upload the Anti-Virus Program from here. You can do this by calling up the program using the [and] buttons, and then pressing \ to upload it.

Hit the five switches on the large panel in this room; however, you must press the switches in a certain order to deactivate the Beam Emitter Shield. Remember the NW - SE - W - NE code? Hit the switches in the following order: top-left, bottom-right, bottom-left, top-right, and center. You must do this rather quickly, though, before they all reset.

Ascend the shaft in this room. This is where the mirror nodes are located. Your task is to rotate these nodes into proper position. You must turn two of the mirrors towards the other shafts, enabling the third mirror to line up with the small, blue megavolt-like charge. You must angle the nodes in every adjacent room like this. When finished, head back down to the room with the Data Link. After all the nodes are in correct order, a large purple "O" will appear on the monitor.

To keep from getting lost, you should probably place a marker in the first mirror node chamber.

Return to the area with four entrances. When you arrive, hang a right. This is the room with the slain body. Descend below until you reach the area with three levels. Descend to the lowest level to see a number of Icons on screens down below. Your job is to align the long arm with the "O."

Tip

Move the long arm by touching the Icons. Each time you bump it, the arm will move clockwise one icon panel.

After doing this, hit the switch to enable the defense network output. After doing so, go to the four entrance junctions. Head through the ceiling shaft, and navigate back to the room with the five puzzle switches. Drop your Gunboys around the beam emitter, the area between the lens chambers and the small blue area at the top of the huge structure in this room.

Note

If you don't place the Gunboys, and you flip on the three switches in the equipment room, the Bots produced from the matcens will attempt to destroy the emitter lens.

Return to the room with the three matcen switches. Upon arriving, head back to the beam emitter chamber. Watch out for the antics of the Thief; it is most dangerous when wearing its Cloak. Touch the CED sign located above the Data Link to get all the wheels in motion.

Help the Gunboys defend the lens from the ensuing robot attack. It's best to stay within the lens shaft as much as possible. Upon uploading the data, you will have finished one of the longest and toughest missions in *Descent 3*. Congratulate yourself!

Mission Fourteen

Mission Fifteen

Dravis may have changed the code, or we may have miscalculated. In either case, the anti-virus didn't work.

We tracked a shuttle that left from the space station Shiva to the surface of Venus. We are convinced that this was Dravis.

You must locate him and find a way to stop the virus.

Objectives

- Repair Energy Centers and Reactor (Optional)

- Locate Dravis' Secret Stronghold

Enemies

- Flak

- Hood

- Tailbot

- Squid

- Gyro

- Sharc

- Thresher

- Hellion

Walkthrough

Switch over to the Automap, and zoom out so that you have a full view of the terrain. Your ship should be in the lower-left corner. The tunnel entrance you're heading to is in the northeast. Switch back and make your way across the hostile terrain. You will encounter a Hood, several turrets, and a few Flaks stationed below. Use your craft's Afterburner, cruising as fast as you can to the cavern entrance without worrying about taking out enemy craft.

Tip

You may have to switch on and off from your Automap to see where you are in relation to the entrance. Just remember to hug the outer canyon wall, past the structured entrance, and you will find the small mountain portal in the northeast corner.

At the entrance are a **Cyclone Missile** and a pink, coral-like marker. Descend below, wary of the critters that wait. Take out the Pests in the first room, the one with the lava falls. Collect the **Power-Ups** and **Homing Missile**.

Take the tunnel, not the door, to the next room. A Thresher will give you a hard time, but you can mop it up with a couple of missiles. Exterminate the pests to the left, and then grab the goodies. Enter the large portal. Axe the Squid, and then collect the **Napalm Rocket** and **Power-Ups**.

Go through the floor portal; it's adjacent to the four fan ducts. Descend down the shafts until you come to a large, heavily protected room. A red Gyro and Sparky, among others, will try to ambush you. Fight them from the opening so that you can take on each one at a time. Otherwise, they will try to sneak behind you. After you finish them off, take the **Full Map Power-Up**.

Mission Fifteen

Exit into the shafts. Take the first right and enter the door down this tunnel. Take out the Bots, and then turn the wheel (the one to your far left). This will drain the lava pool in the left corner of the adjacent chamber. Enter that chamber.

Head down the pool-shaft object. Enter the opening below. Hit the switch so that you can enter the door above. It has some **Power-Ups** and the **Inner Stronghold Key**. Grab them, and then leave. There is an open doorway above, which leads back outside the lava pool chamber, so take it.

Tip

The lava is hot and can quickly cripple your Shields if you're not careful. Although it's hard to avoid a little damage, the smart thing to do is descend into the pool chamber only when the lava is drained to its lowest level.

Head back out the way you came. Take the big door and then hang a right. This will take you to the lava falls room. The exit outside is located in the ceiling. Take out the turret and grab the **Vauss Driver ammo**. As soon as you reach the surface, activate your Automap again. Position yourself so that your ship is in the lower-left corner of the map. Directly to the north lies the next entrance.

Tip

If you want to accomplish the secondary objective (repairing the energy reactor), you will first need to head to the terrain entrance in the middle of the Automap.

Navigate through the mountains so as to avoid the Flaks, because their Mass Drivers are deadly accurate. Take out the turret and enter. Swoop down the entrance. Blast the fan that you come to. Descend, wary of the lurking Hood, and take it out. Continue to the large room below with the matcen and lava pool. There are two doors in this room. One is a dark gray P.T.M.C. portal, while the other is light gray. Take the latter.

Enter the room with caution. The turret attached to the ceiling ahead is a hard hitter. Slip into the area to your immediate right. This way you can watch for sneaky Tailbots who would ambush you. Take out the turret from here with one of your missiles.

Gold Stingers and Orbots are ahead. Blast your way through several tunnels. Descend through the large chamber, cleansing the area of menacing Bots. To the right of this chamber is another opening. Take it, and slip to the small areas to your left and right sides to collect goodies.

Mission Fifteen

Head down the hatch, avoiding the barrage of Bot fire until you descend to a cavern area. This is where the Hellion's lair lies. The Hellion is a machine-beast with turreted tentacles.

There are three ways to take out the Hellion. Napalm weapons work extremely well. You can also take out the Hellion with a barrage of constant missiles and energy weapons, but this method does take a while.

Fulfilling the Second Objective

Note

If you want to pursue this objective, you must do so *before* descending to the Hellion's lair.

Go inside the structured entrance (all the others are just large holes in the mountains) and head forward. Several Tailbots will try to harass you. Handle them, then continue below. You will come to a large, cavern-like room with several entrances. Take the one straight ahead. After blasting several more pests, you should see several switches to your right. These switches, when triggered, produce explosives.

Note

Don't get switch happy just yet. In order to activate the reactor, you will need a replacement fuse.

Head slightly forward until you see the entrance blocked by rocks. Head down to this area, swinging to the left. Take out the Sharcs, then continue down this winding corridor until you come out of a trap door in the floor of a room above. Take out the Bots. Continue down this area until you spot some windows. Blast out one of the windows, and then eliminate the Pests in this lava room. Near the pit is an opening. Inside here is the **fuse**; just watch out for Sparky. Once you get the fuse, head back to the room with the entrance blocked by rocks.

Note

Only the switch to your far right is of any use. The first switch jams and the second one produces explosives that detonate as soon as they are dropped to the floor.

Hit the switch near these rocks to raise the elevator. Go over to the three switches, press the far right switch, and watch the duct nearby materialize an explosive. Using your ship, *gently* nudge the explosive onto the elevator. This will take some practice, but eventually you'll get it. Navigate the explosive into the blockage—Ka-boom! Fly in and insert the fuse to the reactor.

Mission Fifteen

Hidden Missions

Mission Sixteen: Secret Level after Mission Eight

The data cartridge that you picked up contained the location of a secret area that might be worth checking out. We have no information on this location. Keep your eyes open!

If you complete Mission Eight with the Data Cartridge, you'll automatically go to Mission Sixteen.

Objectives

- Find Area 1
- Find Area 2
- Find Area 3

Enemies

- Tailbot
- Stormtrooper
- Gyro
- Orbot
- Sharc

Walkthrough

You're receiving an incoming transmission from the Beagle. Press *F8* and *Shift* to view the message. The Beagle wants you to explore this unknown area. Head through the red door, and then swing left. There are several **Power-Ups**, along with the **Afterburner Cooler**. Now enter the door on your left.

To your right are two Tailbots. Take them out, and then collect the goodies, including a **Super Laser** and some **Concussion Missiles**. A **Full Map Power-Up** is hidden under the platform near the purple number "3." Grab it and leave the room.

Continue to the left and pick up the **4-Pack Missiles** strewn across the corridor. After collecting the last one in this area, look to your left. In this cubbyhole lurks a Tailbot. Smoke it. To your right will come an Orbot and another Tailbot. Axe them too. Continue to the right. You should see a purple number "3" marking along the wall entrance. Head down this corridor.

Note
A floor opening is located within this long corridor, but you can't descend to the chamber below from there.

A room with a red glow is ahead, so enter it. To your right and left are two shafts with plenty of goodies—and quite a few Tailbots. Rush into the right half and take the **Smart Missiles**. The area is a dead end, so you'll have to come back out into the red room. To your left is even more stuff: **Mega Missiles**, a **Microwave Gun**, a **Mass Driver**, and an **Impact Mortar**, among other things.

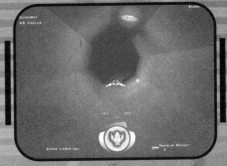

Head back the way you came. Turn right, and look for the purple number "2" tunnel. Take out the Tailbots and Gyros so that you can collect the **Napalm Fuel**, **Napalm Rockets**, and **Frags** in the purple number "2" area. Head back out.

Turn slightly to the right again, looking this time for the purple number "1" tunnel. Right across from the numbered shaft (to your left) is a Tailbot and some Orbots. More Bots will greet you before you find the room. Axe them. This room is loaded with good stuff, including **Seeker Mines**, **Gunboys**, **Fusion Cannons**, and an **EMD Launcher**.

Once you finish adding to your collection, descend to the green, glowing area below. The hidden mission is now complete and your stockings are full!

Mission Sixteen

Mission Seventeen: Secret Level after Mission Twelve

The data cartridge that you picked up contained the location of a secret area that might be worth checking out. We have no information on this location. Keep your eyes open!

To access this mission, simply complete Mission Twelve with the Data Cartridge. This will take you directly to Mission Seventeen.

Objectives

- Destroy Blue Key Force Field Generators
- Acquire the Blue Key
- Destroy Red Key Force Field Generators
- Acquire the Red Key
- Destroy Reactor Force Field Generators
- Destroy the Reactor
- Escape the Research Center

Enemies

- Stormtrooper
- Lots of Turrets

Wakthrough

First things first: place a marker where you begin. After you do that, it's time to get a move on. Although the goodies across from you look tempting, don't rush over there just yet. The large areas to your right and left both have turrets hooked to the floor. Take these out first, and then fill your grab bag.

Note

It's best to take the turrets out at floor level. Rush onto the first one, pounding it with firepower. Weave in and out of the crevices, and then ambush the second turret.

Take a right from the place where you planted a marker. Descend down the wind tunnel, where you will be dumped in a room with another turret. Don't waste your time on it; just send a Cyclone its way. Below is an unlocked door (above the wind tunnels), so enter it.

Take out the two Bots, then destroy the force field generators. There are the six icy blue panels on two sides of the room, and the two pale white mechanisms on the other wall. After blasting them with your lasers, slip down the wind tunnel. Stop when you see some switches. Decelerating is the best method for stopping when you need to. Hit the switches to deactivate the flame-throwers below.

Note

The wind tunnel is fast, so you'll have to be on your guard for the two switches. Rush toward the middle of the shaft, where a "floor" exists.

Mission Seventeen

Take the wind tunnel down once again, but then prepare for a barrage of fire. Two turrets and two Stormtroopers are waiting below. Send some missiles at the turrets, then dust off the Bots. Two small ducts are available for hiding if things get too heavy.

Tip

There are some goodies stashed in the two small ducts, including a Gunboy.

There are two sets of wind tunnels leading down; one is marked with green lights, while the other has white ones. Head down either one of the white tunnels. They lead to a chamber with two turrets and a Stormtrooper. From the floor's pit, take out the Bot, and then pump some missiles into the turrets.

Above this pit is a wind tunnel. Ascend to the next chamber. Acquire the **Blue Key** and ascend to the room in which you began. Go to the other side (left from the marker) and descend below. Shoot out the turret. Descend through the lower door; the other door will open only with the Red Key.

Note

Déjà vu! The tunnels that lead to the Red Key are an exact mirror image of the Blue Key tunnels. You will even encounter the same types of robots.

Take out the two Stormtroopers, then destroy the Red Key Force Field Generators. Go down the wind tunnels with the white lights. Hit the switches to deactivate the flame-throwers in the next room. There's a pit below with two turrets and two more Stormtroopers. You know what to do.

Ascend up the middle wind tunnel. While zooming up the shaft, take out the lurking turret. Collect the **Red Key** and head out along the opening next to the tunnel protected by the blue force field. Take the door with the two orange lights beside it. Go down one of the three green wind tunnels (they all lead to the same room).

To your left and right are two small, orange shafts. Take out the fuses and force field generators along both walls. This will disable the Reactor's Force Field. Inside the next chamber are some Bots. Smoke them and then destroy the Reactor. You can now exit the area.

Chapter Five: Multiplayer

So, you've played the single player game. Well, now it's time for the real deal—hop onto Parallax Online (PXO), Outrage's free game matching service, and mix it up with the best *Descent 3* players from around the world. They're gonna be good, but if you read this chapter you can be better!

Advanced Piloting Techniques

Taking out Gyros and Orbots is one thing, but flying against human opponents is significantly more challenging. Some pilots have been playing since the original Descent released in 1995, and they have more than a few tricks up their respective sleeves. If you want to hang with them you have to fly smart, and you'll need to take a few pointers from the aces.

Triple Chording—Learn It, Love It, Live It

I didn't pay much attention to the vectors chapter in my physics book, but that's fine because Descent taught me all I needed to know. Now I'm going to let you in on it! As you've probably figured out by now, your ship can slide up and down as well as side to side. That "sliding" motion is vertical or horizontal thrust, and if you move forward (or backward) *and* slide at the same time, you'll move faster than if you go just forward alone.

Here's the important part: If you move forward and slide in one direction (up, down, left or right) at the same time, you'll move approximately 1.4 times as fast as if you were just flying straight ahead. The pros call this "double chording."

But that's nothing. If you want to win, you need to "triple chord." To triple chord, you need to slide in two directions (for example, right and up, or left and down) and move forward or backwards simultaneously. A triple chording Pyro can move approximately 1.7 times as fast as a Pyro that's just going straight ahead. That's what you call a tactical advantage!

Learning to triple chord can be tough, but it's a necessary part of any pilot's bag of tricks. If you're using a joystick with a hat switch, simply move the hat diagonally in any direction and move forward or backward. Compensate for the ship's orientation by adjusting your aim.

The Spiral

If you need to cover a lot of ground fast, link your triple chords together in a spiral. For example, start sliding right/down, then move to right/up, then over to left/up, then left/down, etc. Just don't get too predictable; if you fly the same way all the time, other pilots will anticipate your actions.

Burnin'

Combine triple chording with the afterburner and you'll get some serious speed. Don't waste your afterburner though; if you've taken heavy damage and need to get away from a fight but your burner's empty, it's all over but the cryin' and the shoutin'.

The afterburner provides the most thrust from about 100 to 80 percent, so smart pilots will just use the afterburner in short bursts, and let it recharge quickly.

Beyond the Circle Strafe

The single player piloting section taught you the circle strafe. However, if you're a real gamer, you are already a strafing expert. In levels like the Core and Taurus, the circle strafe is a vital dogfighting tactic. On the other hand, in open levels like Half-Pipe and Steel Vapor, you have more options.

Here's a concept for you: the "sphere" strafe. In addition to circling left or right, fly above and below your opponent. This is especially effective if you're in a circle strafe battle and your opponent loses sight of you for a moment. Take that opportunity to fly above or below him and lay the smack down, sight unseen.

Multiplayer

Snake Versus Shadow Fist— Fighting Styles

If Kung Fu movies have taught us anything, it's that some fighting styles are better than others. While there is no Shadow Fist or Drunken Monkey fighting style in *Descent 3* (at least not yet), there are a number of styles you should learn about. No player will rely exclusively on one of the following tactics. In fact, the best players borrow from all of the following strategies. If, however, you can learn the strengths and weaknesses of each particular style, you'll be well on your way to putting a hurt down on the opposition.

The Dogfighter

Dogfighting is close combat with lots of circling, dodging, and weaving. To become an ace, you must master dogfighting. To master dogfighting, you must become an awesome pilot, and you must know which weapon to use in which situation. It's an art, and no amount of reading is going to teach it to you. It's simply something you can only learn through experience. I can tell you what you have to learn, just not how to learn it.

What separates the great dogfighter from the wannabe is movement. A great dog-fighter knows when to start sliding left instead of right, when to close, and when to back away from a fight. He (or she) knows how to dodge his opponent's weapon fire, and how to lead his opponent so that his own weapons hit the appropriate target. Pretty much any primary weapon (with the possible exception of the EMD) can be used effectively in a dogfight. Watch out for old school D1 and D2 players armed with the Fusion—they can take you out with one well-aimed shot!

The Bum Rusher

Some players charge and hope you panic, which is a good tactic for taking out newbies. But then again, just about any tactic is good for taking out newbies. If a player "bum rushes" you, triple chord and afterburn right past him, turn around, and unload your arsenal.

The Tunnel Rat

Tunnel fighters prefer to get up close and personal. They avoid open spaces, and instead rely upon fighting in a tight mineshaft, where one well-placed Frag Missile will do the trick.

These players will fly into a room to get your attention, and then duck back down a tunnel and wait for you to emerge. Don't fall for this trick. Send in some Napalm Rockets, Homing Missiles, and Impact Mortars towards them and cue your "Fire in the hole!" audio taunt.

The Sniper

Snipers like to set up shop with their backs to a wall and a clear view of an open area. Then they set back and wait for any prospective targets. The weapon of choice for the Sniper is the Mass Driver, which can zoom in on faraway ships. In addition, the EMD and Vauss can also inflict some serious damage to an unsuspecting victim.

There's little to do against a Sniper except go after him once he's shown himself. Watch for the telltale trail of a Mass Driver round coming at you from across the level; this is a good indication that you're being sniped. If you can avoid flying straight and level, you'll make the sniper's job much more difficult.

The Camper

Everyone hates a camper, although as long as you're the one doing the camping, it can be kind of fun. Campers enjoy loading up on weapons, setting up an ambush, and then waiting for some hapless pilot to appear around a blind corner.

Camping near a horde of Power-Ups or other attractive bait can be particularly effective, so if you see a lone Shield Power-Up sitting out in the open, watch your back! Camping is excusable if you're tired from a marathon Anarchy session, and just want to take it easy for half a minute. On the other hand, career campers are punks who don't have the skills to dogfight.

The Kill Stealer

Don't be too quick to label someone a "Kill Stealer." That's a slur in the Descent world and, after all, if you happen upon two pilots in a dogfight, you're going to shoot at one of them. If it happens to be the one that was already at zero shields, well, that's the way the game goes. However, if you notice one particular pilot always seems to come from nowhere and get that last Homing Missile shot in on another player you've been working over, you may have a Kill Stealer on your hands. If this happens, there's only one thing to do—hunt 'em down and take 'em out! Then do it again—they'll get the message!

Multiplayer

The Weapon Juggler

These pilots are dangerous. They've perfected their flying skills, and now they're working on the other half of the equation—using the right weapon at the right time. From long range, they can hit an opponent with the Mass Driver or the Vauss. Then when you get closer, the Weapon Juggler can switch to Quad Supers or Plasma, get right up in your face, and finish the job with the Fusion, Napalm or Omega.

If you see a pilot employing these tactics, rest assured that they know what they're doing and you better too if you're going to have a chance.

Playin' Dirty

This section covers some devious tricks to add to your arsenal.

- In large, open levels, fire a long blast of EMD (this sometimes works with Homing Missiles and Megas too) from one end of the level and you're almost guaranteed to catch someone off guard.

- Drop Gunboys in doorways.

- When you have plenty of weapons, fire Blue Lasers at an opponent and duck into a tunnel. Then when they come in after you, greet them with Quad Supers and Smart Missiles.

- Fire a Napalm Rocket or Impact Mortar behind your victim, then hit 'em with the Mass Driver and push them right back into the blast.

- Avoid setting up Gunboys or camping near spawn points. That's just *too* dirty!

- If you're playing a hoard game, don't commit suicide right before you're about to be killed so the other player can't get your hoard orb. That is beyond weak!

Playin' Smart

This brief section details some things to keep in mind while playing.

- Avoid rushing into a big fight armed with Blue Lasers and Concussion Missiles.

- Never fly straight and level.

- Avoid bumping into walls or making noise that will alert other players to your location.

- Don't pick on newbies.

- Avoid getting frustrated at yourself.

- Don't back down from a player who constantly keeps killing you. Learn from your mistakes and from their skill.

Run What Ya Brung

Unlike previous Descent games, *Descent 3* players have three ships from which to choose. Each has its own strengths and weaknesses, and one may be more suited to a particular fighting style than the other two.

Get to know each ship's characteristics so that you know what you're up against. Check your **Ship Config screen** under the **Pilots menu** to switch your own ship.

The Magnum—Big and Bad

The Magnum is devastating in close combat situations. Catch a Phoenix or a Pyro in a tight tunnel and prepare your audio taunt, because that battle's going to be short and sweet.

The Magnum has the toughest shields of any ship, and its weapons pack the biggest punch: the Microwave Cannon, Napalm Gun, and Fusion all fire triple bursts instead of the usual two. Plus, the Mass Driver has a quicker reload time. This ship can carry more ammo and its Quad Lasers fire in a close, tight spread so all four are more likely to connect.

Multiplayer

On the other hand, the Magnum is a big, slow target without much "umph" in the afterburner department. In open dogfights, the Magnum pilot will have a difficult time drawing a bead on the swooping Phoenixes and Pyros. Flown by a pilot who understands its good and bad points, though, the Magnum will rack up the kills.

The Phoenix–fast but fragile

The Phoenix is the ship the aces will choose. That's not to say it's the best, but in the hands of a truly skilled pilot, the Phoenix's natural speed and strong afterburner make it difficult to hit and impossible to catch.

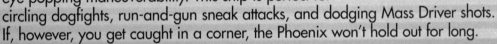

This ship was created to triple chord, however, it's not so good at soaking up damage. Light shields and less potent weaponry is the price you pay for such eye-popping maneuverability. This ship is perfect for circling dogfights, run-and-gun sneak attacks, and dodging Mass Driver shots. If, however, you get caught in a corner, the Phoenix won't hold out for long.

This won't be the ship of choice for missile boaters, those players who join empty multiplayer games and stock up on ammo. The Phoenix can only carry a maximum of two Megas, compared to three for the Pyro and eight for the Magnum.

The Pyro GL–Jack of All Trades

You know it, you love it. The Pyro was, and still is, good at everything. Good for newbies, good for the very best, just plain all-around good. However, the *Descent 3* Pyro GL is now the best Pyro ever—it's faster and has a higher turn rate than the D1 and D2 Pyros. It's quick enough to hang with the Phoenix in an open fight, and strong enough to stand up to the Magnum.

The Pyro's greatest strength is that it has no one great strength. You can dogfight, you can snipe from a distance, and you can change your strategy on the fly and exploit the weaknesses of your opponent. If you're only planning to master one ship, this is the one!

Would You Like to Play a Game?

There are two ways to play multiplayer *Descent 3*—on a LAN (local area network) or over the Internet. LAN games are ideal, because there's far less lag time compared to an Internet game. The problem is if you work in an office with a bunch of other *Descent 3* maniacs (or if you're hooked up to a university network), LAN games can be difficult to organize.

Most multiplayer gaming takes place through hosting services like Parallax Online (aka PXO, **www.pxo.net**), HEAT (**www.heat.net**), or Kali (**www.kali.net**). Regardless of the service you use, you must learn to deal with lag time and packet loss. (See **www.myrkul.org/descent.html** for an excellent FAQ explaining all the technical ins and outs of playing Descent on the net.) But for now, we'll give you a quick rundown on all the things you need to know.

If at all possible, join a game that's running from a dedicated server. "Dedicated" will probably appear somewhere in the game name, or you can press "i" to determine if the game is dedicated or not. Games run by a player who is also the server aren't as fun, because that player will have a significant advantage.

When you see a list of games that you can join on, for example, PXO, you'll see each one has a certain ping. Ping time is the amount of time it takes for information to travel from your computer to the computer that is hosting the game. The lower the ping time the better, and a high bandwidth connection on your side of things will help minimize ping. If you have a ping of .250 (or one quarter of a second), that means a player's ship appearing on your screen is actually a quarter of a second behind its real location. In other words, you need to aim where you would expect the ship to be one quarter of a second later. That's hard. When ping times start to get more than .300 to .500, it's time to switch to a different game.

Conclusion

The single player *Descent 3* game is tough. The folks at Outrage made sure of that. But even the best AI Bot can't match a good human opponent. Unfortunately, there is no trick that will bestow multiplayer prowess upon your wings. It takes practice and it takes knowledge. We've helped with the latter, only you can do the former!

Multiplayer

Chapter Six: From the Horse's Mouth

Many creative and hardworking individuals helped put together *Descent 3*, from programmers and designers to sound technicians and artists. The man who was in charge of harnessing all this talent into the masterpiece we have on the store shelves today is producer Jeff Barnhart. Mark Walker caught up with Jeff, and asked him a few questions about his ideas, life, and the latest installment in the *Descent* series.

Mark: Your job is a lot more than fun and games. Some people may not be aware of what all a game producer actually does. Could you give a brief summary of your duties in *Descent 3*?

Jeff: As a producer, you end up being responsible for everything that relates to the project that you are working on. Your biggest responsibility is to make sure that the game is fun. However, there are a ton of things that need to get done before the game hits the store shelves, and as the producer, you need to make sure it all gets done. You work with marketing on your advertising, your packaging, and anything else, such as $50,000 tournaments. You work with PR for all of your press events and get previews and reviews. QA helps you find bugs, and sometimes you end up packing up and spending the final month of the product living with the developer.

Mark: What is the biggest challenge a producer faces in pulling together a title?

Jeff: The biggest challenge a producer faces is in weighing the pros and cons of improving the game, while working with the time line you have. You can always make something better, but the clock is always ticking. Deciding what to do, and what not to do, is where you really show your skill. You have to know just how significant of an impact it could have on the quality of the game, and how many man hours it could take to get it done. Juggling your schedule, your team, and the quality of your game is what it's all about.

Mark: How did you break into the electronic entertainment industry? How long have you been producing?

Jeff: Long, long ago, I started as a tester. Long hours, hard work, and dedication brought me through the ranks of QA and then onto a team as an assistant producer. I later took on my own titles, and have been producing for the past three years now, which brings me to the pinnacle of my career: getting a chance to work with Outrage on *Descent 3*.

Mark: Do you remember the first electronic game that you ever played? Could you tell us about that particular experience?

Jeff: Pong. My parents couldn't pull me away from the TV.

Mark: Artists often envision their work well before it's completed. What vision and goals did you take to the table when producing *Descent 3*?

Jeff: First off, I knew we needed the best gameplaying experience. Because with everything else aside, gameplay and the experience that we can make the user be a part of is all that counts. I want the player to feel something in his heart every time he flies into a new area, meets a new or old enemy, or gets sent on a new mission. I also wanted to make sure that our multiplayer remained top-notch. Outrage has done a fantastic job with every one of these things.

Mark: *Descent* is a classic, a game that revolutionized the degree of freedom and motion available to gamers. Today, some of the most popular games on the market use similar techniques. Was working on *Descent 3* intimidating because of the original's status? What were the biggest challenges in producing the game?

From the Horse's Mouth

Jeff: Definitely. But in the end, it worked in our favor. We knew that we had to do justice for the *Descent* franchise, and working on something so big has brought out the passion, dedication, and hard work of everyone on the team.

Mark: What elements of *Descent 3* do you consider an improvement from the original? Why?

Jeff: The story-driven levels, the quality of the 3D graphics engine, and the outside areas of the levels are the biggest improvements over the original.

Mark: The AI is astounding. Was that given a high priority in the development cycle?

Jeff: This had one of the highest priorities. What the AI does in a game is one of the most important things a game can have. This is what puts personality into the enemies, and what puts feeling into the player's heart.

Mark: What are some of your favorite games? Did any of them influence you in putting together *Descent 3*? If so, how?

Jeff: A few of my favorite games are *Doom*, *Quake*, *Jedi Knight*, *Zelda*, *Gran Turismo*, and *Half-Life*. I'm sure that every game I have ever played has influenced me in one way or another.

Mark: What is your favorite level within the game, and why? What is your favorite multiplayer option, and why?

Jeff: That's a tough question. I can't really decide. I'm having so much fun with every level right now that I don't think I could choose just one. For multiplayer, I like playing Anarchy games over the PXO. Doing battle with other pilots and getting your stats tracked is awesome!

Mark: There are a number of Robot bad guys in *Descent 3*, many with their own distinctive personality. Which ones are your favorites and why?

Jeff: The Henchmen on Level 4 are one of my favorites. These are guys that fly ships just like your own, but the ships are black. I have fun with these guys because fighting them is just like fighting real people; their AI is really good.

Mark: Do you have any advice for gamers who want to pursue a career in the industry?

Jeff: Just do what you love and things will fall into place for you. If you want to work in the game industry, devote your life to playing games and having fun. You will eventually meet the right people, and they will help you get started.

From the Horse's Mouth

Index

P

PB-5 Pest, light walker, 59-60
Pests, 120–121
Phoenix, 76, 197
piloting strategies, 15–22
    multiplayer games, 191–192
Plasma Cannon, 80, 158
playing dirty, fighting, 195
Priest Icon, 123–124
primary weapons, 77–81
programmer interview, 201–204
Pyro GL, 197
Pyro GL player spacecraft, 75

Q–R

Quad Lasers, 97, 126

R-1 Security Pass, 98
Rapid Fire Power-Up, 97
RAS-1 Gyro, light flyer, 26
RAS-2 Tubbs, medium flyer, 34-35
RAS-3 Stinger, heavy flyer, 47
Red Acropolis, escape, 114
Red Stinger, 20
Restricted Access Passkey, 93
review mirror, 141
RM-10 Flak, medium roller, 65-66
RM-15 Tracker, medium roller, 67
robot generator, 134
rollers, 64-67
RR-47 Tailbot, medium flyer, 41

S

Scratches, 109
Secret Areas, 133, 135, 153
Secret Door, 123
secret level, 185–188
Secret Rooms, 103
Seeker Mines, 121
Seekers, 120
Seismic Disrupters, 139
Seismic Stabilizer, 138
Seoul, 107–112
SH-1100 Thresher, heavy flyer, 49-50
Sharcs, 170

Shield Power-Ups, 96
Shield Recharging Center, 164
shields, 21–22, 90
shuck and shoot, 18–19
SK-1 Sickle, medium flyer, 36
Smart Missile, 85
Sniper fighting technique, 194
spacecraft, players, 75–76
Sparkys, 18
speed, 17
spiral, piloting technique, 192
SPT-99 Hunter, light flyer, 28
SQ-90 Squid, medium flyer, 39-40
ST-55 Watcher, light turret, 70-71
Stormtroopers, aim and, 21
Super Laser, 7, 121, 126
Supply Depot, Mission Two, 97
surveillance cameras, 151–152
SW-9 Juggernaught, heavy walker, 61
SX-66 Hellion, heavy flyer, 52

T

Tailbots, aim and, 21
Thiefbot, 105
Torture Mechanism, 156
Train Station, 109
triple chording piloting technique, 191–192
Tubbs, 92
tunnel rat fighting technique, 193–194
tunnels, 98
turrets, 69–72, 102, 126

U–V

UFO machines, 120

Vauss, 116
Vauss Cannon, 78
Vauss Rounds, 116, 121
Virus Containment Device, 130

W–Z

walkers, 57–62
weapon juggler fighting technique, 195
weapons, 75–86

Fallout 2

A POST NUCLEAR ROLE PLAYING GAME

Sequel to the RPG of the Year

KILL SMARTER, NOT HARDER

Improved combat AI for friends and foes alike. Most of the people in your own group won't take that burst shot with the Flechette–gun, but a couple are probably just aching for the opportunity.

BIGGER & BADDER THAN EVER

Bigger, smarter, nastier enemies than you've ever fought before. We've given you a few pals that are just as ugly. You didn't think you were the only bad-ass in town did you?

LEARNING IS FUN-DA-MENTAL

Over 100 new skills, called perks, available to learn during the course of your travels. Better to learn the exquisite art of Pyromania, the uncanny timing as a Demolition expert, or how to squeeze the trigger on your spiffy new Gauss-rifle faster than the next guy? Decisions, decisions...